The Heroic

Saint Francis Xavier

PATRICK J. LOBO

"Nihil Obstat"
Sd. /- Fr. Manuel Pascoal Gomes
'Censor Deputatus'
Church of St. Francis Xavier
Borim, Ponda P. O. Goa, 6/11/2014

CP / 4646 / 2014
'Imprimatur'
Archbishop's House, Panjim, Goa 6/11/2014
+ Filipe Neri Ferrão
Archbishop-Patriarch

© Patrick J. Lobo 2014

Cover and book design:
Nisha Albuquerque
www.nishaalbuquerque.com

Photo credit:
Agnelo Lobo
www.lobodigitalgoa.com

Paintings:
Wikimedia Commons
Google Art Project

Old photographs and maps:
Brordrick, James, Saint Francis Xavier (1506-1552)
Schurhammer, G, Francis Xavier: his life, his times, 4 volumes

ISBN: 978-93-84298-12-8
Price: 495/-
First published 2014

© Published by

BROADWAY PUBLISHING HOUSE

SIGNATURE STORE:
1st Floor, Ashirwad Building, Near Caculo Island, 18th June Road, Panjim, Goa
Tel: +91-832 2420677, 6647037, 6647038 | Fax: 6647038
Email: bbcbooks@rediffmail.com, info@booksingoa.com
Website: www.booksingoa.com

Printed by Rama Harmalkar +91-9326102225

Contents

Foreword

Fascination for St. Francis Xavier, affectionately called *Goemcho Saib*, has intensified down the ages. His paradoxical life, in the words of one of his biographers "a kaleidoscope of quickly-changing patterns and contrasting, and even contradictory attitudes", rather than clouding the heroism of the saint, contributed towards more and more people delving into the depths of his personality. From the ramparts of the ancestral Castle of Javier, where he was born, to an isolated hut in Sanxian, where he breathed his last, with his wishes to go to China unaccomplished, betrayed and alone, St. Francis remained intrepid amidst fiercest of oppositions, situations, abuses and persecutions. His achievements in these parts of the world have been spectacular and they underline more the lights than the shadows in his life; or rather, the shadows make the lights shine brighter.

"The Heroic St. Francis Xavier", an addition to the plethora of publications by a youngster, is one more perspective on this hero who left a mark in the landscape of this region of Asia and the Fareast. He writes extensively about his missionary challenges he bore and the fruits yielded for God's Kingdom, no doubt; yet, the framing of the journey inside the long journey of humanity to its promised land launches the reader in that journey and calls him to enter into that "Joy of the Gospel," which Pope Francis says, that "fills the hearts and lives of all who encounter Jesus", the Joy that sets free those who accept his offer of salvation from sin, sorrow, inner emptiness and loneliness (*cf Evangelii Gaudium 1*). Imbued personally with this spirit, as a catechist he is, Patrick J. Lobo, the author of this well presented book, does this by evoking the great events and figures from the Economy of salvation and giving us the monumental magnificence inspired by the trails St. Francis left and the faithful expressed through art and architecture. This goes to underline the research involved in this work. His dedication to the proclamation of the Good News to tiny tots stands out in these pages: text and photography.

After reading this work, no one will remain indifferent to this great saint whose body remained incorrupt for quite many years but today reduced to remains. Yet his message goes beyond his grave. St. Francis, loyal to the Society of Jesus which he co-founded together with St. Ignatius of Loyola and some companions, never lost sight of their motto *Ad Majorem Dei Gloriam*, "to the greater Glory of God." And this is indeed the aim of every follower of Christ.

Fr. Francisco Caldeira
Chapel of S. Tomé
Panjim, Goa

Prologue

The first book of the Holy Bible, Genesis, symbolically describes the Spirit of God, taking the formless void and darkness, sweeping over the face of the waters of earth, active in creation of the earth and the first human being. Since that beginning, the work of the Holy Spirit of God is visible: firstly, in the Old Testament; then, during the times of Jesus, where He was conceived by the Holy Spirit, baptised by the Holy Spirit, and anointed to preach, perform miracles, die on the cross and rise from the death by the Holy Spirit; and from the Pentecost till the end of time, the Holy Spirit lives amongst us. The three Dispensations in the history of the Bible refer to: the Old Testament as the Age of the Father; the Gospels as the Age of the Son; and from the Pentecost onwards as the Age of the Holy Spirit.

Pentecost was the Jewish "feast of the weeks" traditionally celebrated on the fiftieth day after Passover. On the tenth day after resurrection of Christ when the disciples

Pentecost, by Jean Restout II, 1732

St. Peter, by Peter Paul Rubens

and followers were gathered to celebrate the feast of Pentecost in Jerusalem on "Mount Zion", suddenly there came a sound from heaven, as that of a rushing mighty wind and instantly many tongues as of fire appeared above the heads of the disciples and slowly dropped down and rested upon them and they were filled with the Holy Spirit including other believers in Christ. After receiving the Holy Spirit they were filled with divine power and began to speak in different languages which were not known to them and were heard by thousands of Jewish pilgrims who flocked to celebrate the Pentecost.

Saint Peter

Peter, one of the prominent followers of Jesus, filled with the divine Holy Spirit stood up and gave the first sermon. He said that these people are not drunk as you think, because it is only the third hour of the day but this is what prophet Joel had prophesised: God had promised to pour out his Spirit on all flesh, empowering diverse people to exercise divine power.

The evangelisation, ministry and missionary works started on the Mountain in Galilee when the resurrected Jesus gave the great commission to his disciples: *"All authority in heaven and on earth has been given to me. Therefore go and make disciples of all nations, baptising them in the name of the Father and of the Son and of the Holy Spirit, and teaching them to obey everything I have commanded you. And surely I am with you always, to the very end of the age." (Matthew 28:16-20 NIV)*

St. Paul, Philippe de Champaigne

The disciples received the Holy Spirit and the great commission from the resurrected Jesus and they started preaching, evangelising and baptising. The community of the first apostles and the followers of Jesus began the first church and St. Peter was head of that church.

Saint Paul

Paul, the eminent Apostle, was chosen by the risen Christ for his missionary journey on the Damascus Road when he was on his way to persecute early Christians. He was Saul of Tarsus, who was converted to Christianity and renamed Paul. He was destined to be a missionary. Paul made three missionary journeys preaching the gospel, building churches, encouraging the early Christians in Jerusalem, Asia Minor, Greece and Rome. He preached the Gospel not only to the Jews but also to Gentiles. Out of 27 books in the New Testament, 13 are attributed to Paul as the author.

St. Peter and St. Paul were martyred in Rome under Emperor Nero in the year 87: St. Peter was crucified head downwards and Paul was beheaded. The Church unites them in common celebration giving them identical honour. The Divine Holy Spirit continues to dwell in the followers of Christ and empowers them to continue the ministry of Jesus.

Saint Francis of Assisi

In the 13th Century, St. Peter, the rock on which the Church was founded, and St. Paul, the missionary who was destined to preach the gospel to the Gentiles, appeared to St. Francis of Assisi when he was praying and praising the virtues of holy poverty. The connection of St. Paul with St. Francis of Assisi goes deeper. St. Paul at the end of the letter to the Galatians says: "I bear on my body the marks of Jesus". St. Paul received the Stigmata, which means the bodily marks which correspond to the crucifixion wounds of

St. Francis of Assissi, by Cigoli

St. Francis of Assisi in Ecstasy, Caravaggio

Jesus Christ. St. Francis of Assisi experienced stigmata in La Verna, Italy in 1224. This is well documented and accepted by the Church authorities as authentic.

St. Francis of Assisi was born in the year 1182 in the town of Assisi in Italy. His father, Pietro Bernadon, was a very rich and wealthy cloth merchant and his mother was known as Pica. Francis was handsome, joyful and soft at heart. Born into a rich family, his companions came from noble families. He was educated in maths, poetry and music, learned to read and write in a school which was a part of the Church of Saint Giorgio of Assisi. Francis was acknowledged to become a cloth merchant like his father and did not plan any further studies. A life of wealthy ease lay before him.

When Francis was twenty, a fight broke out between the town of Perugia and Assisi. He was forced to join the forces of his town. Since the Perugians defeated the Assisians, Francis along with others was taken prisoner and kept in captivity for a year. The sickness in the jail turned his thoughts towards Eternity. While praying in the chapel of Saint

Damiano outside Assisi, he heard a voice from the crucifix telling him to repair the house which was in ruins. Hurriedly, he sold his horse and some garments from his father's shop and gave the money to the priest at Saint Damiano.

Francis' father was furious that his son was wasting money on churches and beggars and took him to the bishop. During the proceedings and hearing, Francis took off all his clothes, gave them to his father and pronounced that he recognised only the Heavenly Father. From then onwards, he lived his life without money and family bonds.

The determination to follow Christ in poverty changed him to give up his old ways and habits and set himself to serve God. He gave money to the poor, begging and distributing clothes and lived the Gospel in its true sense: he not only preached the gospel following all that Jesus said but lived by it without limitation and self importance. Francis lived in a cave for almost two years, praying and meditating. The spirit of the Lord was active in his life though his friends mocked him and his father rejected him. Francis preferred to live his life like a beggar; he loved creation, the birds and beasts and most of all, poverty. He was called the little poor man of Assisi. The Gospel he lived made an everlasting imprint on St. Ignatius of Loyola.

Ignatius of Loyola (militant)

Saint Ignatius of Loyola

St. Ignatius of Loyola was born in 1491 at the castle of Loyola in the Basque province in northern

The Conversion of Saint Ignatius Loyola, by Miguel Cabrera

Spain. He was the youngest of 13 children and his mother *Marina Saenz de Licona y Balda Maria* died when he was child and his father *Don Beltrán Yañez de Oñaz y Loyola* died when he was sixteen years old.

At the age of sixteen, Ignatius was sent to serve as a page to Don Juan Velasquez, as the Royal Treasurer. At the court, he developed the liking for beautiful women and fancy dressing. He was addicted to gambling and was often engaged in swordplay.

There was a dispute between the family of Loyola and another family. Ignatius with his brother and relatives ambushed some clerics for the other family and had to flee to another town. When Ignatius was brought to justice, he escaped the punishment with the defense that he was just a boy. Since his family was very influential, he was exempted from prosecution.

The ambition of Ignatius was to become a knight, and he became one. At the age of 30 in 1521, the French army attacked the fortress at the town of Pamploma. The Spanish soldiers were trying to defend the town but being weak, the army was ready to surrender except Ignatius of Loyola. With zeal and courage, he was ready to defend the fortress and tried to convince the soldiers. But his dreams were shattered when a French cannonball wounded one of his legs and broke the other. Admiring the courage of Ignatius, the French, instead of taking him to prison, brought him to the Castle of Loyola, his family home, for recovery.

Ignatius' legs were set but they did not heal properly - one leg was shorter than the other. This was unacceptable to Ignatius, so he ordered the doctors and surgeons to reset it. He submitted himself to cut his flesh again without any anaesthesia. The doctors gave up hope of his recovery as he was weak and without any strength; he could not take food and was approaching death but on the eve of the feasts of St. Peter and Paul, Ignatius showed signs of recovery and began to grow better.

During his recovery, he was confined to bed and was bored, and wanted to read. He asked for some romance novels. Unfortunately, there were none. So they gave him two books entitled *The Life of Christ* by Ludoph and *The Golden Legend*, a book on the life of saints by Jocopa De Voragin, both in Spanish.

Though Ignatius was dreaming how to impress the illustrious lady he was in love, and how he should journey to the city where she resided, the Holy Spirit was at work. While reading *The Life of Christ* and the books on *The Life of Saints*, he gradually started changing his life and dreaming about the holy life instead of earthly leisure. The Holy Spirit had by now already captured his soul.

While reading these books, he was astonished at the two prominent followers of Christ, St Francis and St. Domnic. He started thinking of following in the footsteps of St. Francis of Assisi. He reflected on how St. Francis of Assisi lived the Gospel in its true sense; at times he felt empty and dissatisfied while daydreaming about the lady. Meanwhile,

Glory of St. Ignatius of Loyola, by Peter Paul Rubens

he experienced the difference between what made him sad and what gave him inner peace and happiness. This was his first reasoning for spiritual exercise. Here, he learned the powers of discrimination and decision making and realised the Sprit of God was drawing him towards an entirely new life.

While recovering from his wounds, he was experiencing inner healing. He gave up his old fantasies and desires and illustrious plans of romance and worldly conquests. He left the castle in March, 1522, headed towards Jerusalem so that he may live in the land where Jesus lived. He travelled through the town of Montserrat where he came across a Benedictine Monastery west of Barcelona. In front of the statue of the Virgin Mary he hung up his sword and dagger as a symbol of his abandoned ambitions.

He continued his journey to Manresa, where he lived in a cave near river Cardoner for the next ten months with prayer, fasting, self-denial and austerity. In the cave he began actually to write the *Spiritual Exercises*, which is a set of meditations, prayers and other tasks to enrich oneself spiritually for a period of thirty days. On the bank of the river, Ignatius had a vision which was an enlightenment. He was filled with the grace of God after the vision, found God in all things. He never revealed exactly what the vision was.

From Manresa, he travelled to Italy and finally to Rome where he met Pope Adrian VI and took permission to make a pilgrimage to the Holy Land. When he arrived at the Holy Land he wanted to stay there, but he was denied the permission to stay in the Holy Land by the Franciscan Superior who was then the authority over the Catholic community primarily because the Turks were the rulers of the Holy Land. Ignatius was also threatened with excommunication, and was forced to leave. Ignatius left the Holy Land.

He returned to Barcelona in March 1524 with a desire for priesthood. He started learning Latin grammar along with young boys under Jerome Ardevoll. After studying Latin for some years, in 1526 he went to the University of Alcala de Henares. Here he gathered many students and others and started explaining the meaning of the Gospel and speaking about prayer. As this was not acceptable to all, he was arrested and detained for almost forty two days. He left Alcala and went to Salamanca to continue his further studies.

Immediately he went on the street to preach but was imprisoned by the Dominicans at the University, suspecting him of heresy; but finding no fault in him, he was allowed only to teach poor children.

On 2 February 1528, Ignatius decided to go to Paris to study at the University of Paris. His subjects were Latin Grammar, Literature, Philosophy and Theology for almost seven years. Each year during summer he would beg for alms from the rich Spanish merchants in Flanders. In 1529 he began his studies at Sainte-Barbe and shared the room with Peter Favre and Francis Xavier. He made known his thoughts to his roommates: how he intended spending his life for the salvation of souls. Since Favre was also having the same thought, he became the first Companion of Ignatius.

Xavier was not keen and was still dreaming about worldly honour. But with much difficulty Ignatius managed to convince him. There were other Spaniards desirous of priesthood too. He recruited James Laynez, Alphonsus Salmeron, Nicholas Bobadilla and Simon Rodrigues and directed them through the *Spiritual Exercises*.

Ignatius along with six companions decided to take the vows of chastity and poverty, and to go to the Holy Land. If it was difficult to go to the Holy Land, they decided to go to Rome and place themselves at the disposal of the Pope. They waited for almost a year. However, the ship was not available to take them to the Holy Land because of the conflict between the Christians and Muslims. Since

Ignatius of Loyola, Church of Gesù, Rome

there was no ship, they started service in the hospitals and started teaching catechism in various cities of northern Italy. This was the time when Ignatius was ordained priest but did not celebrate the mass for another year because his wish was to celebrate his first Mass in Jerusalem in the land where Jesus lived.

Ignatius and two of his companions, Peter Favre and James Laynez, met Pope Paul III. The Pope was impressed with them and gave them the work of teaching scripture, theology and preaching. Here, on Christmas morning Ignatius celebrated his first Mass at the church of St. Mary Major in the Chapel of the Manger.

Since the idea of going to Jerusalem was dropped, Ignatius asked all of his companions to come to Rome to discuss their future. After discussions and prayer, they decided to vow obedience to the superior general who would hold office for his life time, and they would place themselves at the disposal of the Holy Father to travel anywhere the Pope desired. Besides the vows of poverty, chastity and obedience, their main aim was preaching, hearing confessions, teaching the doctrine and caring for the sick. The traditional order of praying the Divine Office in common and other prayers and penances was omitted.

On 27 September 1540, Pope Paul III gave approval to this new Order who addressed themselves as the Company of Jesus: in Latin *Societas Jesu*; in English it became known as the Society of Jesus. Through ballot, Ignatius was appointed by the group as the first Superior of the Society though he was reluctant to accept the position. At the Church of St. Paul in April 22, 1541 all the companions pronounced the vows of the newly formed Order.

Ignatius as Superior General of the Society of Jesus sent his companions for the service of the Lord all over Europe and around the world. He wrote nearly 7000 letters to his fellow companions while communicating with them and keeping them united.

As a student in Paris, Ignatius had suffered from ailments of the stomach and became worse when he was in Rome. In 1556 his health started deteriorating. Though the physician thought that he would survive the summer, Ignatius knew that it was coming to an end, so he told Polanco who was assisting Ignatius to write the letters to get the Pope's blessing but Polanco refused, giving excuse that he would go the next day. At midnight Ignatius' illness became very serious. Polanco rushed to the Vatican to get the papal blessing but it was too late. Ignatius departed resting his soul in the hands of God.

St. Ignatius was canonised by Pope Gregory XV on 12 March 1622 together with St. Francis Xavier. His feast is celebrated on 31 July, the day when he died. St. Ignatius left a legacy of *Spiritual Exercises*.

The *Spiritual Exercises* are collections of meditations, prayers and mental exercises which are divided into four weeks to enrich the relationship with God. It is mostly known as

a "long Retreat" which extends for a period of 30 days. It helps retreatants to attune to God's will in their lives and to motivate themselves to follow the will of God. There are many retreat houses which are conducting much shorter retreats based on the pattern of the *Spiritual Exercises*.

St. Ignatius achieved a milestone when he converted the co-founder of the Society of Jesus, St. Francis Xavier, who was his close companion, a great missionary and evangelist who travelled across the world, blessing and baptising thousands of people. Francis Xavier reinforced the vision of St. Ignatius of Loyola and the Society of Jesus. He shines as one of the most inspiring role models of the Post-Pentecostal Ministry.

Ignatius of Loyola with his companions, Bom Jesus Basilica

Birth and Youth of Xavier

Francis Xavier was born on 7 April 1506 in the castle built in the 10th century located in the hill town of Navarre in Spain. The castle belonged to the noble Magdalena first became a lady-in-waiting to Isabel la Catolica, Queen of Castile and later she entered the convent as a novice of the Clarisas Nuns in Gandia, eventually

Castle of Xavier

family of Javier in the kingdom of Navarre, present day northern Spain. He was the fifth child of Juan de Jasso and Maria de Azpilcueta de Aznarez y Xavier. The little child was baptised at the parish church of Santa Maria which was close to the castle. The other children were Magdalena, Ana, Minguel and Juan.

rising to the position of abbess of the convent. Ana married Diego de Ezpeleta, Lord of Beire. The three brothers evinced their enthusiasm for the profession of arms: Minguel became the future lord of Javier and Juan became a warrior knight who actively opposed the Castilian capture of Navarre.

Interior of Xavier Castle

Francis who was the fifth child and was brought up within the four walls of the castle, received his basic education at home with his mother and the parish priest. He was piously brought up, very carefully trained in book learning. He was enthusiastic and a good learner; he was innocent, pleasing and beloved of all. He witnessed two events which disturbed him during his childhood which had grave consequences on the family of Xavier.

Navarre was invaded by the Fernando el Catolico, King of Castile, in 1512. Juan de Jasso, their father, collaborated with the new invading monarch till he died, three years later, sad and dejected. But Minguel and Juan took up arms to defend the Navarre dynasty in 1516 and 1521 but failed on both occasions. During this period the fortifications, towers and the battlements of the castle of Javier were pulled down. Only the family residence was left. The two brothers of Francis later accepted the pardon in 1524 and returned to their castle home.

When Francis was 19 years old, he decided to follow in the footsteps of his father, Juan de Jasso, who had studied in the University of Bologna in Italy, with a Doctorate in Law and was holding the highest position in the administration of the last king and queen of Navarre. In 1525 Francis bade farewell to his mother and brothers and decided to go to France, to study at the University of Paris.

Francis at the University of Paris

In Paris, Francis took admission as an undergraduate with the introductory course in Humanities, Latin Grammar, Rhetoric and Poetry in the College of Sainte-Barbe. This contemporary University, founded by Lenormant, was a conglomerate of various monasteries, churches, stores, wine shops, etc.

Life at the college campus was lively and noisy as there were students of different faculties, Philosophy, Arts, Theology, Law and Medicine. The rules and regulations were strict: the first lecture started at five soon after the Morning Prayer; at six, the chaplain offered the mass in the chapel where all the students took part along with books in their hands. Some of the students assisted the mass under the supervision of the regent. After breakfast, the classes continued till ten with questions and discussions till eleven. Thereafter the students went home and the residents took meals with the principal

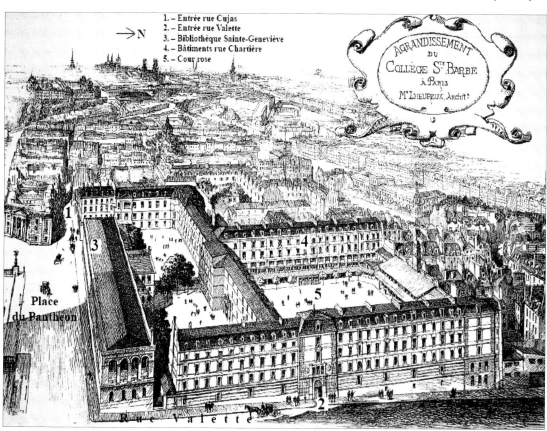

1. – Entrée rue Cujas
2. – Entrée rue Valette
3. – Bibliothèque Sainte-Geneviève
4. – Bâtiments rue Chartière
5. – Cour rose

AGRANDISSEMENT DU COLLÈGE Sᵗᵉ BARBE à Paris Mᵗ LHEUREUX, Archᵗᵉ

Sketch of the College of Sainte-Barbe

Sketch of Peter Faver

and the regents. Classes resumed at three in the afternoon and concluded at five in the evening.

Francis passed the Latin examination on 1 October 1526 and began his course of Philosophy under another master who besides teaching was also undergoing a course in Medicine. He shared the room with the master and another student, Peter Favre. Francis wore a black gown with a leather belt.

Peter Favre was not from a wealthy background and struggled in his life tending his father's sheep on the French Alps. He was simple in nature, studious, and intelligent, with an extraordinary memory. He had made a vow of chastity consecrating himself to God. After initial studies, he was sent to the University of Paris and began studies in Philosophy under Juna Pena. Both Francis and Favre had the desire to acquire knowledge and a rare gift for study. Together they did their four and half years in Humanities and Philosophy and passed their B.A. in the year 1529. Though Francis was shattered, sad and broken, later in the month of July when his mother died in the castle of Javier, he persisted in his studies and in the year 1530, was conferred with a Master's Degree (M.A.) which enabled him to lecture as regent to the younger students, while continuing his theological studies.

There was another student who joined Francis and Favre at the College of Sainte-Barbe, at the University of Paris - Ignatius, who was thrown out of the students' hostel for not paying the fees. Francis and Favre knew about Ignatius being a former soldier, intensely spiritual and with a habit of begging alms. Ignatius was 38 years old when he joined the college whereas Francis and Favre were 23 years old.

Ignatius was full of the Holy Spirit. He had spent years as a courtier and a soldier;

and as a convert, wandered to Rome and the Holy Land to attain his goal to follow Jesus Christ. He started guiding Favre in his spiritual matters at the right time when he was plagued by scruples and was troubled by sexual fantasies. Favre in turn tutored Ignatius in Philosophy. Ignatius helped Favre to understand his conscience and ultimately led him to *Spiritual Exercises*. Ignatius won over Favre completely. He became the first Companion.

Francis was not too fond of Ignatius' ridiculous way of life. At one point of time Francis went through financial difficulties because of high expenses he incurred owing to inflation to achieve his Master's Degree. At Navarre, his brother even thought of calling him back as they could hardly afford the expense of his upkeep. His sister Magdalena, the poor Clare nun from Valencia intervened and stopped the family from recalling him, as she had faith that her brother would one day become the servant of God. Ignatius took advantage of this situation, and started supporting him financially; he even paid for the lectures of the students of Francis and also started increasing the number of his pupils. By this time Ignatius knew Francis well and had seen the qualities in him, therefore he wanted to win him

Lay out plan of the College of Sainte-Barbe

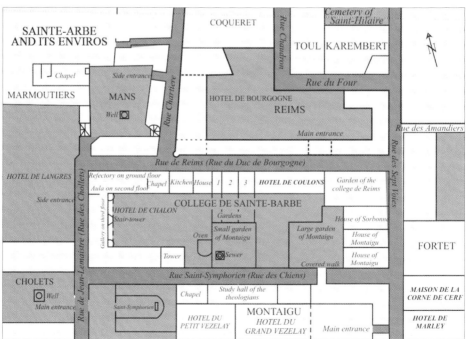

Ignatius and Francis at the College

over. But Francis was still full of worldly ambitions and was very difficult to convince. Although he started enjoying the company of Ignatius, he was not ready to change his lifestyle.

Ignatius was strong-minded and wanted to convince Francis and win over his heart. He started talking about spiritual subjects and other Gospel-related matters. Very often Ignatius used to quote "For what does it profit a man to gain the whole world, and forfeit his soul?" He used this phrase repeatedly to mould the heart of Francis.

Stubborn he was but slowly and gradually Francis started melting; he started to see emptiness in worldly greatness and started realising, thinking and finally, the

sturdy soul was overcome by the power of the Holy Spirit. Ignatius started guiding him to give up the earthly desires to follow Jesus.

Ignatius had by now five more disciples and on 15 August 1534, the day of Assumption, the seven resolved to take a vow to dedicate their lives to the Divine Master. In the Church of Montmartre near the gate of Paris, Peter Favre celebrated the mass when all the seven consecrated and pronounced their vows to follow Christ in poverty and chastity.

First vows at the Church of Montmartre

Journey to the Holy Land

After taking the vows at the Church of Montmartre, Francis then performed the *Spiritual Exercises* for thirty days under the guidance of Ignatius. He was the last in the group of Ignatius Companions to perform the *Spiritual Exercises*.

the University. At this point Francis also received a message from Spain regarding his nomination to a Canonry at Pamplona. But nothing stopped Francis and his companions from going to Venice to join Ignatius. On 15 November 1536, Francis

The Church of Montmartre

Francis spent twelve years in the University and was about to take the degree of Doctor in Divinity. Francis and Peter Favre were highly valued at the University for their outstanding and scholarly achievements. Many were of the opinion that they should stay at

along with his companions left Paris for Venice. They sold their belongings and gave the money to the poor, keeping some for their journey.

The third Italian war between Charles V and Francis I was raging, so the group

Pope Paul III

decided to take a longer route for safety. Clad with long dresses and hats similar to Parisian students, with pilgrims' staffs, leather satchels on shoulders along with the Bible and a Breviary, rosaries around their necks and the manuscripts which contained theological notes, they were ready for departure.

En route to Germany and Switzerland, they underwent many sufferings and turmoil over snow-bound roads and across steep mountains, fearlessly facing the dangers. They finally reached Venice in 1537. Ignatius was there awaiting them. Francis started to work in the Hospital

of Incurables, looking after the sick, dressing their wounds, sores, making their beds.

They served in the hospital for two months, and thereafter set out on foot to Rome to take the necessary permission from the Pope to make a pilgrimage to the Holy Land. Ignatius stayed behind. Travelling on foot, encountering many difficulties and endless troubles, begging for alms along the way, they finally reached Rome on Palm Sunday, 25 March 1537 and stayed in the hospitals of their own nations. When Pope Paul III heard that the group was theologians from Paris, he invited them for discussion over dinner regarding some theological understanding along with some of the Roman Doctors. The Pope was impressed and was delighted with their theological knowledge and humility. He gave them permission and considerable alms to go to the Holy Land but he also cautioned them that they may not accomplish their goal because of the war brewing between Venice and Turks. He also gave them sacred orders to be ordained at the hand of any Bishop they might choose.

Unfortunately, the journey to the Holy Land was abandoned and the pilgrims returned to Venice.

The Call and the Parting

On reaching Venice with considerable alms, they immediately resumed their work of charity at the Hospitals. Soon they renewed their vows of poverty and chastity at the hands of the Papal Nuncio residing at Venice, Monsignor Girolamo Veralli, who was also Archbishop of Rossano. On 24 June 1537, the feast day of St. John the Baptist, Ignatius, Francis, Laynez, Bobadilla and Condure were ordained by Vincenzo Negausanti, Bishop of Arbe but did not offer their first mass on the very same day; they decided to offer the first Holy Mass at the Holy Land.

The prediction of the Pope regarding the war between the Turks and Venice became a reality and it was certain that they could not sail to the Holy Land that year. Their dreams of offering their first mass at the Holy Land were shattered. However, they dispersed themselves in two's or three's to the neighbourhood of Venice and prepared themselves for the first mass.

After about two months, Ignatius called his companions at the old ruined monastery at Vicenza and Francis celebrated his first mass on 30 September 1537 along with Ignatius and the others. Owing to excessive traveling, suffering and weakness and living the life of poverty, Francis and Rodrigues fell seriously ill and they were admitted to the

The Church of Trinita dei Monte, Rome, by François Marius Granet

Hospital of Incurables, sharing the same bed, suffering and consoling each other. In the hospital, Francis had a vision of St. Jerome, to whom Francis had great devotion. Francis came to know that he must serve the Lord at Bologna. Ignatius and others decided by lot where they should go and work as priests: Ignatius, Faver and Laynez went to Rome; Francis and Bobadilla to Bologna.

Ignatius along with his two companions, Laynez and Favre arrived in Rome on November 1537 and met the Pope, who welcomed them and appointed Favre as a lecturer in Positive Theology and Laynez in Scholastic Theology in the University of the Sapienza. Ignatius kept himself occupied in conducting the *Spiritual Exercises*.

Ignatius summoned all others to Rome where they were staying in the city near the Church of Trinita dei Monte in a haunted house. During the Easter of 1538 all gathered in this haunted house and Ignatius made known his thoughts of establishing their society into a religious order. Though Ignatius had formulated the conception of this at Manresa, he did not disclose it. He let the Holy Spirit guide them in its establishment. The Pope gave them authority to preach and hear confessions. In winter while they were in service of the Lord preaching and labouring in Rome, a severe famine struck the city and thousands could have died hungry and with disease, but the companions took charge of one large building with thousands of poor and started caring for them by begging for necessities.

They laboured for several months in the year 1539 with prayer and serving the poor. On 15 April 1539, they signed a document and pledged that they will enter the Society once it was approved, and owing to the fear that they may be accused of forming a Society without the permission of the Holy See, they dispersed separately. They remained in prayer and submitted the relevant documents to the papal office for approval. The Pope was initially not in favour of another religious order and hesitated. But not to discourage them, gave the verbal approval on 3 September 1539. Francis Xavier by the time had left Rome, leaving the company of Ignatius and others for ever. Formal approval of the New Order was given by Pope Paul III on 27 September 1540 by signing the bull *Regimini Militantis Ecclesia*. Since then they referred to themselves as the Company of Jesus: in Latin *Societas Jesu* and Society of Jesus in English. Ignatius was elected as the first Superior of the Society.

From Rome to Lisbon

Once the Society was formed they started their missionary work in different places. Francis was nominated as a Secretary to Ignatius and kept up the correspondence with the members and became the chief letter writer of the Society. At the end of the fifteenth century, the Age of Discoveries was started by two countries situated on the Iberian Peninsula: Spain and Portugal. In the fifteenth century, the sea was seen as a dangerous, mysterious and fearful challenge. Spain and Portugal found many brave men willing to explore the dangers of the sea with their own motives and desires for trade, wealth, glory and to spread Christianity.

The Portuguese nobleman, Vasco da Gama, sailed from Lisbon in 1497 with the mission of exploring a new sea route for trade towards East. After sailing down the western coast of Africa and rounding the Cape of Good Hope, he reached India at Calicut on 22 May 1498. Within the next half a century they sailed all over the Eastern seas, exploring new trades and spreading civilisation and Faith.

King John III, born in Lisbon, who was the fifteenth King of Portugal, also called the Grocer King, reinforced his bases in India and particularly in Goa for the spice trade. He was more concerned with

Portuguese Vessels

evangelisation and spreading the Gospel truth in the extreme East. Govea, once the Superior of the College of St. Barbara at Paris, was now the trusted adviser of the King. Govea had written to Ignatius regarding the need of missionaries to spread the Gospel to the East Indies. The King instructed his ambassador at Rome to request the Pope to deploy at least six missionaries. On request of the Pope, Ignatius decided to give only two priests.

The first, Simon Rodriguez who himself was a Portuguese from a noble family. He had returned from Siena and was suffering from fever but nothing could stop him. He took along with him as companion, Father Paul of Camerino. Bobadilla, who was then labouring in the kingdom of Naples, was the second choice.

Mascarenhas, the ambassador, was waiting for departure along with Bobadilla to Portugal, when Bobadilla reached

Parting of Francis

Rome. Just before the departure of the ambassador, he fell so ill that he was unable to travel. The ambassador could not wait nor travel alone and could not go to Portugal without the missionary. There was no one else to replace Bobadilla except Ignatius and Francis.

Ignatius called his secretary, Francis. Though reluctant to part with his right hand, he had no choice. He told Francis that by the order of the His Holiness two of them had to go to the mission in India. Since, Bobadilla could not travel owing to his illness and the ambassador could not wait, Francis at once offered himself for the mission to India. Without wasting much time, he took the parting blessing

King John III

of Pope Paul III, embraced Ignatius for the last time and set forth for the journey to Portugal.

Before leaving, he placed in the hands of Laynez, his companion, a sealed envelope. It contained three declarations. First accepting all the rules and constitutions which should be made by the Society, the second contained his vote for Ignatius as Superior of the Society, in case of his death, for Peter Favre to be chosen, and the third, the vows of perpetual poverty, chastity and obedience for the superior.

The ambassador of Portugal, Pedro Mascarenhas, and Francis began their journey from Rome to Portugal. Francis was well aware about the opening of the Portuguese domain in India. He was ready to serve the Lord in the vast field which was open to Apostolic Labourers. The journey he made was much more comfortable than the earlier ones: he had travelled this road from Loreto to Rome about three years ago. He made a short visit for the last time in the Holy House of Nazareath. Francis heard the confession of the ambassador on the Palm Sunday in the Church of Our Lady of Loreto and thereafter reached Bologna where they were received with enthusiasm for he had laboured there over two years and the memories were vividly fresh. He

stayed with the pastor of Santa Lucia and departed after thanksgiving mass.

Within two days they reached Parma, where Favre and Laynez were working. He surprised Laynez in the Hospital of San Cosma e Damiano but could not meet Favre because he had gone out to console the sick. The route was not favorable and prone to accidents because of snow and difficult terrain. Francis came to the rescue of the Secretary to the Ambassador who stumbled over a stone and fell from a great height. After several efforts, he could not be saved. When Francis arrived at the spot and saw the helpless man, he risked his life and saved him from death. They reached near Pamplona, the beloved capital of Navarre, where his family castle was located and where his aged old mother lived. Francis had not seen her since he left Paris. He could have taken the opportunity to see her for the last time but to the surprise of all, he completely self denied himself the temptation. He was burning with fever to spread the Gospel to India. Finally after three months of journey they reached Lisbon on June 1540.

On the very same day as soon he arrived at Lisbon he went to meet Simon, who was then suffering from quartan fever. Francis was glad to see him and embraced

Audience of Francis with the King of Portugal

him. With the joy of the union, Simon did not get the fever almost a month and was healthy. After they arrived in the city, the King received them with kindness and great pleasure. The King with the Queen held an interview: for almost an hour the King inquired about them and their Institute. During the audience the King also introduced Infanta, his daughter and the Prince Royal, his son, and discussed about the children. The King was pleased with Francis and ordered all young gentlemen of his court to make a weekly confession. He was of the opinion that if these young men knew "God and served Him" they would be perfect examples for others; if his nobility were reformed, the state will be reformed in turn.

The King was pleased with Francis and the society; so he supported the interest of the Society. He had also made secret inquiries about their way of life and wrote to the Pope to expedite approval of the Society and entrusted his pages under spiritual care. Francis immediately started his work as he had done at Venice, Bologna and Rome: attending the sick in the hospital, visiting the prisoners, catechising the children and performing *Spiritual Exercise* for principal persons in the court. Since Francis had refrained from preaching in the churches and was less involved in public actions, the King asked him to preach as he wanted to hear Francis' sermons. The Bishop of Lisbon was also of the opinion that he should not refrain from public exhortations.

His maternal uncle of Javier, Martin D' Azpilcueta, a doctor of Navarrre was the first professor of divinity in the university of Coimbra. On hearing of his nephew's arrival at Lisbon, he requested His Majesty to send him to him promising two lectureships, one in canon law and the other in mystical divinity. He even promised to follow him to India but Francis refused his uncle and turned down his request, considering his age, to go with him to India. The King was desirous to provide everything possible in his capacity for Francis and his companion. The visible and wonderful change the missionaries brought to the court and the kingdom was so great that they were regarded as extraordinary men, full of the Spirit of God.

Within two months, Francis and his companion won the heart of the King and people so much that the people were of the opinion that they would lose two zealous priests if they were sent to India. Francis even informed his beloved Superior Ignatius about the peoples' desire to not let him depart for India. The King thought it would be best for both the missionaries to stay in his kingdom than to go to foreign nations; he hoped that they would bear more fruit in a Catholic country than among barbarians. The opinion of the King was approved by all except by Don Henry who argued that they were nominated for the mission to India by the Vicar of Christ and opposing it was an interference with the Order of Providence.

To resolve the matter, they wrote to Rome to the Pope and to Ignatius. The Pope refused to take the decision and referred the whole affair back to the King. However, Ignatius, though informed that the two priests were at the disposal of the King, to satisfy all he suggested to retain Rodriguez in Portugal and permit Francis to proceed to India. Francis was overjoyed as he was once again chosen for the eastern mission. When the time came for the departure, the King called Francis and discussed with him at length regarding the conquered countries and requested him

Departure port of Portugal during the time of Francis

to visit the places where God was served and to communicate to him if anything was lacking for the establishment of Christianity. He also ordered Francis to write to him frequently.

The King thereafter presented Francis four briefs, which the King himself procured from Rome. In two of them, the Pope appointed Francis as Apostolic Nuncio, with ample powers to extend and maintain the Faith throughout the East. In the third and fourth briefs, he recommended him to David, Emperor of Ethiopia and to native Princes to give him special care and protection from the Cape of Good Hope to the East of the Ganges.

Before they embarked on the ship for the voyage to India, the King ordered Don Antonio D' Ataida, the supervisor of the naval stores, to give whatever he wanted for his voyage and to assure that everything was provided to Francis for the Journey. But politely Francis refused to take anything. Since the King was insisting, Francis asked him for a few books of devotion which he thought would be useful in India and a thick cloth habit to protect himself against excessive colds. Surprised by this, the Count urged him to make better use of the King's offer but Francis politely refused. Finally, they insisted that he cannot refuse the attendance of a servant which was a necessity. Francis replied "As long as I have my hands, I will have no servant." Observing the dignity of his character, Francis promised to uphold the decency of the Count. Francis further said, "As long as I do nothing sinful, I am not apprehensive of scandalising my neighbour nor misusing my authority given by the Holy See, I have nothing to fear". The Count had no reply, and could not say anything.

The time of the embarkation came and Francis went to the port along with two members of the Society, who were to journey with him to India, Father Paul Camerino, an Italian, and Francis Mansilla, a Portuguese, who was not yet ordained as a priest. Simon Rodrigues escorted Francis to the fleet and embraced him with tenderness and Francis said: "These are the last words I shall ever address to you. We shall see each other no more in this life. Let us suffer the separation with patience, and be convinced that, if we be united in the Lord, we shall commune with each other; and that nothing can separate those who are united in Jesus Christ". He further told him the meaning of the dream where he cried one night: "I will reveal to you a secret that I have hitherto kept concealed. You may remember that when we lodged in the same chamber in the hospital at Rome, you heard me cry out one night: 'Yet more, O Lord, yet more'. You have often asked me the meaning of this exclamation; and I have always answered that you should not trouble yourself about it. I will now tell you that I then beheld, whether sleeping or awake, God only knows, all I was to suffer for the glory of Jesus Christ. Our Lord infused into me so great a love of sufferings that, not content with the troubles which were presented to my imagination, I asked to suffer yet more. This is the meaning of these words, 'Yet more, yet more, O Lord', which I then uttered with such fervor. I hope that Providence will grant me to suffer in India, what He has foreshown me in Italy, and that the desires with which he inspired me, will be shortly satisfied."

It was his thirty-sixth birthday on 7 April 1541, and the ship *St. James* sailed. Don Martino Alphonso de Sosa, Viceroy of India, was onboard along with Francis, and was glad that he was having the company of Francis.

Portuguese map of India

From Lisbon to Goa

Christianity in India is traced way back to 52 A.D. when it is believed St. Thomas landed at Muziris which is now known as Cranganore, near Cochin and preached the Gospel, converted many natives and established about seven churches. The second significant coming of Christianity was ushered in with Vasco da Gama's discovery of the route to India on 20 May 1498. He landed at Calicut which is today known as Kozikode. He was born in 1460 in the coastal town of Sines and was appointed by King Manuel to be a Captain-Major for the expedition to India in search of Christians and spices in the year 1497.

Goa was then a part of the territory of Yusuf Adil Shah, Sultan of Bijapur. He had captured the city from the Bahaman empire. Goa at this time became an international centre of Trade between different countries; it established relations with all the trading nations in the East. Goa made a marvellous progress. Many significant palaces, mosques and temples were built in those glorious days. But Goan society was groaning under the Muslim ruler. There were wars and quarrels between the Mohammedans and the local Kings. The inhabitants were longing for an end to the disturbing times and for normalcy to be restored.

Afonso de Albuquerque captured Goa on 25 November 1510, and gradually started introducing his own administrative system. He established the *Senado de Goa, Fazenda, Alfandegas, Casa da Moeda* and other administrative buildings. A friar of the Dominicans; Domingos de Souza, was the first to enter Goa but the first seeds of Christianity and Evangelisation were sown by the Franciscans in the year 1517. They dedicated themselves to the works of the Apostolate. The founder of the order was St. Francis of Assisi.

Francis Xavier's ship *St. James* set out from Lisbon on 7 April 1541. After navigating for a few months, the crew and the travellers reached Mozambique which was the kingdom of the eastern coast of Africa, inhabited by black and barbarous people, who carried their trade with Ethiopians and Arabs. There was no secured port so they halted a mile's distance from the mainland. The sick were immediately brought to the hospital which the Kings of Portugal had founded on the island. Francis too followed them and immediately started his ministry and visited all the sick in the hospital and administered to them with the last sacraments and gave medical remedies to some. Francis fell ill with fever and many were of the opinion that he should leave the hospital. One fine day he met a physician, who told him that he is extremely ill, more dangerously than others. He advised him to take rest and not labour until his fever subsided. Francis took more care of himself and his fever gradually disappeared but his strength was not restored to normal.

After about six months in Mozambique, they re-embarked on the 15 March 1542.

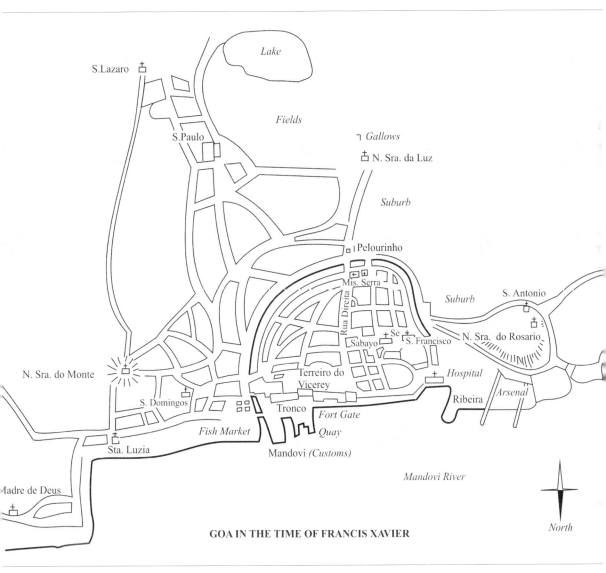

GOA IN THE TIME OF FRANCIS XAVIER

Lay out plan of the city of Goa during the time of Francis arrival

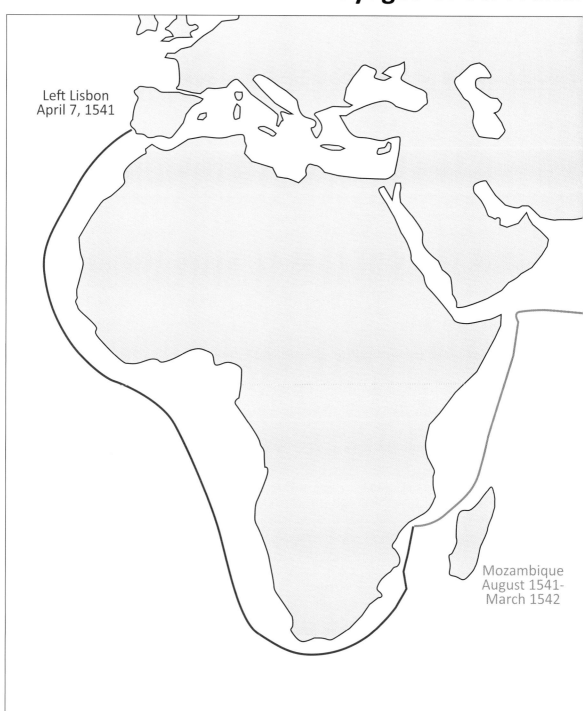

Left Lisbon
April 7, 1541

Mozambique
August 1541-
March 1542

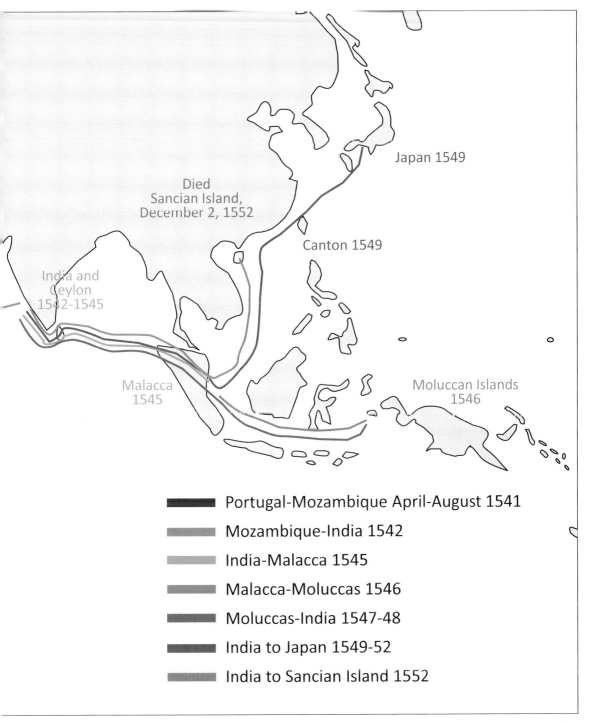

Japan 1549

Died
Sancian Island,
December 2, 1552

Canton 1549

India and
Ceylon
1542-1545

Malacca
1545

Moluccan Islands
1546

▬▬▬ Portugal-Mozambique April-August 1541

▬▬▬ Mozambique-India 1542

▬▬▬ India-Malacca 1545

▬▬▬ Malacca-Moluccas 1546

▬▬▬ Moluccas-India 1547-48

▬▬▬ India to Japan 1549-52

▬▬▬ India to Sancian Island 1552

Francis baptising Indians, by Luca Giordano

A few days later, Francis and the crew arrived at Melinda, on the African coast and then reached Socotra. This island was earlier captured by the Portuguese but abandoned for the lack of local provisions and owing to the unhealthiness of the place. Francis found a number of Christians but most of whom were not baptised. Francis was sad and his attention went towards them. He baptised many infants and wanted to stay there for some time. He requested the Viceroy to let him remain on the island but the Viceroy did not approve, and told him that as the Providence had designed him for India, it would be unfaithful to his vocation. He humbly submitted to the Viceroy.

They finally arrived in Goa on 6 May 1542. The journey lasted for twelve months and thirty days since their departure from Lisbon.

The Bishop of Goa was then an old Franciscan friar, John Albuquerque, a holy man and his jurisdiction extended to the whole of India and the Portuguese settlements in the East. A Franciscan friar, Diego de Borba, who was the disciple of John of Avila, was there in Goa for almost four years and had accomplished much and had founded many associates for the benefit of Indians. A college was also founded at Goa through his efforts and many native Indians were educated with the intention that they would become Priests or at least catechists for their own countries. The college was supported by the Governor and all assistance was given for its existence. This college was later called Santa Fe and thereafter the College of St. Paul.

On landing at Goa, Francis took his residence at the hospital as usual but did not start his missionary functions. He visited the Bishop of Goa and informed him of his mission from the Pope and the King of Portugal, and also informed him that he was appointed as Apostolic Legate and presented the papal briefs. Nonetheless, he made it clear that he was not intending to use the extraordinary powers which were conferred upon him by the Pope and the King of Portugal without the consent of the Bishop.

The Bishop was astonished with the simplicity of Francis and at once embraced him with great tenderness. He kissed the Papal briefs several times and gave them back to Francis and uttered these words. "An Apostolic Legate, sent by the Vicar of Jesus Christ, needs not receive his mission from any other hand. Freely use the power conferred on you by the Holy See; and be assured that if the Episcopal authority be necessary, it shall not be wanting to you." From this point onwards Francis had a close friendship with the Bishop.

Though the Portuguese extended their domain in India and Far East and converted many to Christianity, the Portuguese and the native converts lived sinful lives: uncontrolled wastefulness prevailed and polygamy was openly practised. The evil of slavery was on the rise and even the female slaves were freely sold. The crimes had increased and most of the time the offenders went unpunished. The Portuguese and the natives started amassing unlawful wealth and extortion was publicly professed. The Bishop of Goa was helpless. Though he threatened them with the terrors of God's justice, and the censures of the ecclesiastical tribunals, the culprits were not ready to change.

When Francis saw the sinful practices followed by the Portuguese and the natives he wished to apply a remedy to all of them at once. He thought of bringing reform, immediately starting with the Portuguese. If the Portuguese lived their lives as per the will of God, it will be a perfect example to the converted natives to follow. He spent several hours at night in prayer, and slept only for four hours, frequently broken to administrate the sacrament. He stayed in the public hospital and in the morning after his prayer he celebrated Mass. In the forenoon, he visited the public hospitals, especially that of the lepers which were at the suburbs of Goa and collected the alms from door to door and distributed them to the needy. He visited the prisons and thereafter in the evening while returning he went to the town ringing a bell and inviting the children and the slaves for catechism. He was of the opinion that if the Portuguese youth were well-instructed in the principles of their religion and inculcate in a devout life, Christianity would soon be revived in Goa. He brought the children to the church and taught them the Apostle's Creed, the commandments and other basic prayers. The children started getting attracted towards the teaching of Francis. They began to change their lives and became religious, modest and devout.

Francis began to preach in public and his sermons were attended by numerous people, he spoke with the power of the Spirit of God and minds of the sinners were changed. The catechetical instructions were so impressive and effective that the Bishop ordered that henceforth children should be taught the Christian doctrine in all the churches of the town. Dedicated to his mission and with the power of the Sprit of God, Francis reformed the city, where the people gave large sums of money to Francis, who in turn distributed them publicly in the hospitals, prisons and to the needy.

Map of India Depicting Fishery Coast

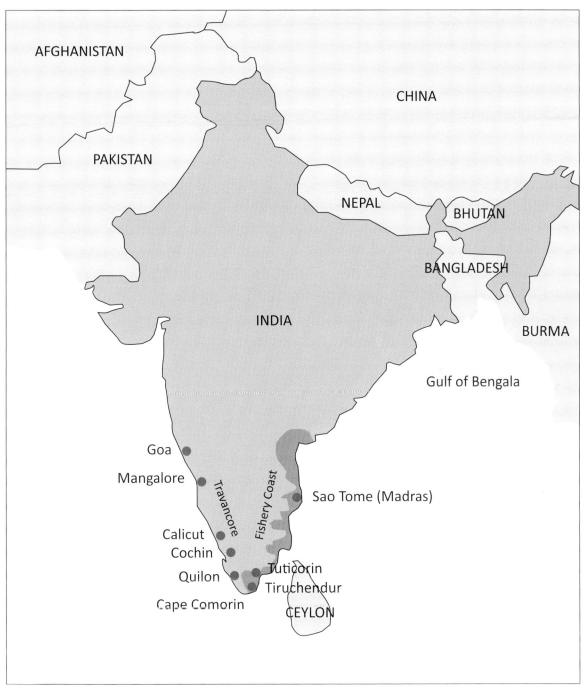

Francis in the Fishery Coast

The fire of preaching the Gospel within Francis was growing; he wanted to spread the Good News as far as possible; adventurous Francis was ready to travel to any part of the world for the love of Christ. The Fishery Coast falls within the coastal area of southern India and it extended from Tuticorin to Comorin. The whole of this coastal area is known as the Fishery Coast because of the presence of pearls on the coast. The natives of this coast were the Paravas who were low in caste and poor.

The Paravas were Christians by name for almost 13 years but they were never instructed regarding Christianity. The Vicar-General of Goa, Minguel Vaz, a zealous man, wanted to propagate the faith on the Fishery Coast. So he told Francis that there are many avenues to spread the Gospel among the Paravas. He told Francis that to complete the conversion would be an act acceptable to God but did not force him because the heat was not tolerable during the fishing season and the land was barren,

Paravan village of the Fishery Coast

The chapel above the cave of Francis at Manapad

not suitable for life. Only the merchants frequented the Coast for the pearls.

Francis, always a man in a hurry to serve his Lord, at once offered to go and instruct the abandoned people. He took the Episcopal benediction and embarked on October 1542 in a small vessel, taking along with him two clerics who were familiar with the Malabar Language. Soon after landing he came across a Manapad village which was largely occupied by idolaters and were not ready to become Christians. Though all the neighbouring villages had been converted, the lord of their territory was reluctant and had forbidden his people to become Christians. Several efforts to convince them were in vain and Francis faced failure.

There was a woman in the village in pain of labour with so much difficulty and helpless. The natural remedies nor the native prayers could help her to deliver the child. Francis with one of his companions visited this sick woman. In one of his letter to Ignatius, he describes: "I went with one of my companions to the sick woman's house and began with confidence to call upon the Name of the Lord, forgetting that I was in a strange land. I thought of the text, 'The earth is the Lord's and the fullness thereof, the compass of the world and all that dwell therein.' So I began, through an interpreter, to explain to her the articles of our religion and the mercy of God. This woman believed what we taught her. At last I asked her whether she wished to be a Christian. She replied that she would gladly. Then I recited a Gospel over her. It was the first time I suppose that such words had been heard in those countries. I duly gave her Baptism. Not to make a long story, immediately after

Baptism this good soul, who had put her hope in Christ, and believed, was delivered of her child; and afterwards I baptised her husband, his children, the infant and all the family."

The word of the miracle spread all over the village and Francis continued preaching the word of God to the natives but they were not ready to become Christian and to embrace Christianity without the permission of their prince. There was one officer in the village collecting annual tribute on behalf of the prince. Francis took the opportunity of meeting him and expounded the law of Jesus Christ to him so meaningfully that he at once acknowledged the preaching of Francis and permitted the inhabitants to embrace it. The chief people of the palace, with

Manapad, the centre of St. Francis Xavier's apostolate

St. Paul's College, Goa

their whole households, were the first to embrace the faith; the rest followed their example, and so all of every class and every age received Baptism.

Francis was overjoyed and encouraged. The fire was burning in his heart to proclaim Christ to as many souls he could and came to Tuticorin. This was the first town actually belonging to the Paravas. They were baptised only because of the favour granted by the Portuguese to expel the Moors from their region. With two of his interpreters he started announcing the truths of faith, but could not achieve much as the instructions through the interpreters were not effective. Francis designed a plan to counter the barrier of the language. He called some of the people who knew the Portuguese language and along with the two interpreters, successfully translated the sign of the cross,

the Apostle's Creed, the commandments, the Lord's Prayer and whole of the basic catechism.

He took a bell in his hand, assembled the children and started teaching the Christian doctrine. The children easily learned most of the prayers as they were instructed in their own language. He repeated the prayers several times along with them and they started learning and enjoying. He also instructed the children to teach their parents and others. His efforts were so effective that he started understanding and speaking the Malabar language.

After almost a year of tireless work on the Fishery Coast, Francis returned to Goa in December 1543 and met his companions Paul Camerino, Diego Fernandez and Francisco Mansilas who were left behind at Mozambique. The Governor of Goa had appointed them at the St. Paul College. Francis received three mails from Europe, the first letter was from Ignatius and the other two were from Rodrigues. Through these letters, he learnt that on 27 September 1540 Pope Paul III had granted official recognition to the Society of Jesus, and Fr. Ignatius de Loyola was elected Head of the Society. Francis was overjoyed and renewed his solemn religious vows in the hands of Bishop of Goa.

Francis Leaves for Travancore

Since Christians at the Fishery Coast had increased, he had engaged a number of people and children to continue the good work. Francis remained a short time in Goa and set himself again to go to the Fishery Coast. The harvest was big but the labourers were few. Francis along with Francis Mansilla who had arrived from Mozambique and who was not yet ordained Priest, and two native Indian Priests went to the Fishery Coast. On arrival, Francis taught them how to convert the natives. After assigning them their role in the proclamation of faith,

Francis baptising the natives

he moved further on towards the east of Travancore which was densely inhabited. Travancore in modern day is central and southern Kerala.

At Travancore, with the influence of the Portuguese, he took permission from the King of Travancore to publish the law of God. He used the same methodology as on the Fishery Coast and the whole of the coast was converted to Christianity. He baptised about ten thousand at once and within a short time founded forty-five churches in Travancore. He found easier to propagate the faith at Travancore. It is said that whenever he made any converts, he first erected a cross and next a booth of branches and palm leaves which in time was replaced by the church built with stone and cement.

Francis started preaching the Gospel to the Mukkuvas, and this time he started talking in both Tamil and Malayalam though he had never learned these languages. He preached many a time for five to six thousand persons together in an open place. Meanwhile the Brahmins laid a trap to murder Francis as they could not tolerate his overwhelming success. They shot several arrows at him but only one wounded him slightly. He narrowly escaped. They started searching him and even set fire to three or four houses. He

St. Francis Xavier preaching for the natives

village on the sea coast were terrified looking at the army approaching towards them. They immediately spread the news at the court about the invasion.

The King of Travancore was most powerful among the kings of Malabar; he put his troops together to defend the kingdom. When Francis heard the news about the invaders approaching, he fell on the ground and prayed: "Remember, O Lord! that thou art the God of mercies and the protector of the faithful. Give not up to those ravening wolves, the flock of which thou have made me pastor. Let not these Christians, who are as yet young and weak in the faith, have reason to repent for having embraced it; and permit not the enemies of thy Holy Name, to oppress those who confide in thy protection."

was forced to hide himself for a whole night in a tree.

The Badages, a tribe of savages and public robbers had made inroads into Travancore and plundered and robbed many places. They were against Christians. They came from the border of Cape Comorin, were well-armed and in military order. They made their advance to the village of the poor fishermen; the inhabitants of the

After the prayer he stood up and with the power of the Holy Spirit without any fear, took with him a troop of fervent Christians and holding a crucifix in his hand, ran towards the marauders who were advancing for the battle. When he came in between, he stopped and cried out in a commanding voice: "I forbid you, in the name of the living God, to pass further; and bearing His authority, I command you to return by the way you have come." The enemies were terrified, fearful and motionless; they panicked in

Miracle of St. Francis Xavier, dead man brought to life

helped to convert the entire kingdom to Christianity.

When Francis was preaching in Coulan, a maritime village of Travancore, he found that there were many people attached to their ancient superstitions. They acknowledged the gospel but were not ready to give up their old practices. Francis was disheartened and prayed fervently for the conversion of their hearts. He raised his eyes to heaven and shed tears and asked God to have pity on them. Since they were not ready to believe his words, he asked them at least to believe in his works. Francis remembered that a dead man was buried the previous day, and addressed to them with a fervent voice "Open the sepulcher, which you closed up yesterday, and bring out the body. Observe first whether he who was buried, be really dead."

face of the commanding presence of the mysterious person. The whole army with the shock of his fearlessness, turned back and left the field of battle.

The people who accompanied Francis were astonished and went to the neighbouring villages and narrated the event. The King of Travancore who was called the 'great Monarch, called Francis and said "I am called the 'great Monarch', henceforward you shall be called the great Father. Acknowledging, Francis told the King that it was only because of Jesus Christ, and that he himself was only a weak instrument, incapable, by itself, of doing any good. The King ordered to publish an edict in the kingdom and commanded all to obey the "Great Father" and subjected himself to embrace Christianity and called Francis his brother. The miracle of Francis

The dead body, which was showing the sign of putrefaction, was taken out from the grave and was laid at the feet of Xavier, near the burial place. Francis knelt down, and after a brief prayer, he addressed the dead body: "I command thee in the holy name of the living God to arise, for the confirmation of the religion which I announce. At once the dead man arose with perfect health. All present at the event cried in a loud voice that whatever

St. Francis Church, Travancore

Father announced was true and fell at his feet and asked him to baptise them. At the same coast, Francis raised another young Christian, who had died of fever. The parents of the deceased, who were most eminent, were accompanied by many relations and distinguished people of the country. When they saw Francis, they fell at his feet and begged him to restore their son. Francis prayed, and made the sign of the cross on the corpse and sprinkled it with holy water and taking the young man by the hand commanded him to rise in the name of the Lord. The corpse immediately came to life. The parents were overjoyed and in memory of this they immediately erected the cross on the site where the miracle was performed.

Voyage to Mannar and Ceylon

The news of the gospel he preached and the miracles he performed at Travancore spread to the neighbouring countries. The people of Mannar Island heard about Father Francis and sent some deputies, inviting him to visit their country. The island of Mannar is located between Ceylon and the Fishery Coast. It was described as a sandy land which was not very fertile with one good port and considerable traffic. Mannar was a small kingdom. He even wrote several letters to Ignatius in Rome and Rodrigues in Lisbon about the need for missionaries. In one of the letters, he expresses his feelings, " I have often thought of running over all the universities of Europe, especially that of Paris and of crying aloud to those who abound more in learning than in charity: 'Ah how many souls are lost to heaven through your fault!' Would that these men applied themselves as zealously to save souls as they do to acquire science. Then they might render to God a good account of their learning and of the talents they have received from Him. Under the influence of thoughts like these, many would make a spiritual retreat, and meditate on heavenly things in silence that they might hear the voice of God. They would renounce their passions, and, trampling on all worldly vanities, would prepare to follow the impulses of the Divine Will. They would say from the bottom of their hearts: 'Behold me in readiness, O my Lord; send me wheresoever thou shall please, even to India if thou dost command it'."

Francis wished that he could go to Mannar but was busy at Travancore and was not ready to abandon the infant church. He sent a priest whom he had left on the Fishery coast. The labours of this missionary bore fruit with the benediction of heaven many became Christians. The isle of Mannar which was the northern part of Ceylon, present-day Sri Lanka, was under the dominion of the King of Jafanatapan which was the northern part of Ceylon. The prince of Jafanatapan heard the news that there was conversion and that the people of Mannar became Christians. He immediately ordered his army to go to the island and to execute all the Christians. The army went to the island of Mannar and slaughtered all the Christians without any discriminations of age or sex. Before execution, they examined them separately; if they were ready to renounce their faith they would be saved. The inhabitants of the island bravely submitted themselves to death. About six to seven hundred laid their lives for the name of Jesus Christ. The entire place is consecrated by the holy blood and is named 'Pasim' which is therefore called 'field of martyrs'.

Miracle of St. Francis Xavier, by Peter Paul Rubens

The motto of killing was to eradicate converted Christians; however, with this persecution, Christianity started flourishing.

There was a young prince at the kingdom of Ceylon, who was secretly instructed by a Portuguese merchant, who was frequently visiting the court. However, the king came to know that the Prince was preparing to receive baptism, put the prince to death and cast his body naked as food to savage beasts. The Christian merchant buried the body in the night. In the wee hours in the morning there was a cross formed which covered the corpse of the martyr. The next day there appeared another vision of a red light cross over the grave.

The sister of the King had privately embraced the faith and instructed both her son and nephew. She ordered the Portuguese merchant to take them to a seminary of Goa. This merchant cleverly succeeded and escaped from the island and went to Travancore to meet Francis. As soon as the King of Jafanatapan heard that his son and nephew escaped for Jesus Christ, he was furious and ordered some of his messengers to bring them back dead or alive but he was not successful. Francis was informed about these circumstances, and he taught it

would be better to dethrone the king and give the throne to the rightful owner. The Portuguese were determined to punish the king, the merciless persecutor of the Christians.

Francis recalled Mansilla from the Fishery Coast, submitted him the Church of Travancore and left for Cambaya to meet the Viceroy of India. Francis had two motives for this journey: firstly, that of the king of Jafanatapan and secondly the Europeans in India who were living irregular lives. He arrived at Cochin on 16 December 1544 and met Micheal Vaz, the Vicar General of India and explained the purpose of his journey and tried to convince him regarding the weakness of the government. He said, " Don Alphonso de Soza was, indeed, a religious man but he lacked vigour; and that it was not sufficient to mean well, unless evil-doers were resolutely and strongly opposed. He added that it was necessary that the king of Portugal should be informed of all the disorders that prevailed in India by one who was an eye witness of them, and whose integrity would be above suspicion. Vaz agreed with the views of Francis and set sail to Portugal. Francis gave a letter to John III, "Your majesty ought to be assured, and frequently call to mind, that God has chosen you among all the princes of the earth, for the conquest of India,

Painting, Francis preaching the Gospel

St. Francis Xavier baptising the natives

Portuguese employed in the government of India and suggested to him to put a stop to the disorders conducted by the Portuguese. He further recommended in his letter "that when God shall summon your Majesty to judgment, a thing inevitable, and which will happen, when you least expect it, you may hear from him those words: 'Why did you not punish your officers, who made war on me in India; you, who were wont to punish them so severely when they were negligent in collecting your revenues?' It will not avail you anything to say in reply to Jesus Christ: 'Lord, I recommended yearly, by letters to my subjects, all that concerned Thy honour and service.' You will undoubtedly be answered: your orders were never executed; and yet you permitted your ministers to act as they pleased.'

that he might try your faith, and see what requital you would make Him for all His benefits. You should also consider, that in conferring on you the empire of a new world, He did not so much intend you to fill your coffers with the riches of the east, as that you should display your zeal, by making known the Creator and Redeemer of the world to the idolaters, by means of your servants."

He then explained the good intentions of Michael Vaz and the conduct of the

"I therefore implore your Majesty, by the fervent zeal you have for God's glory, and by the care you have always manifested for your own salvation, to send here a vigilant and efficient minister, who shall direct all his actions to procure the conversion of souls: who may act independently of the officers of your treasury, and not suffer himself to be led astray, by the policy and worldly-minded men, who regard nothing else than the profit of the state. May your Majesty be pleased to inspect your revenues from India, and then see what expenses are incurred for the advancement of the religious; that when you shall have weighed all things well, you may see if what you give bears any proportion to what you receive. You will, then, perhaps, find that you have just ground for fear, lest you should only have given an inconsiderable pittance to God, in return for the immense treasures He has heaped upon you."

The letter was so convincing that Michael Vaz negotiated with John III, and convinced him to appoint a new governor and came back with orders and decrees, signed by the king.

When Francis arrived at Cambaya, he went to meet the Viceroy and expressed his sentiments regarding Jafnapatan. Sosa was convinced, and immediately dispatched couriers to the captains of Cape Comorin and the Fishery Coast to assemble all their forces at Negapatan and to capture alive the Murderer of Mannar and to bring him to Francis, who desired not his death, but his conversion, and who hoped that the blood of the martyrs of Mannar might obtain for him the forgiveness of his crimes.

Francis stayed at Cochin for almost three months and then set sail to Negapatan where the Portuguese kept their fleet ready. As he passed through the island De las Vaccas, near Ceylon at Saracen on his way, he raised a dead child to life. He then visited Mannar island where he went on shore and kissed the ground blessed with the blood of the Martyrs of Pasim. When the Manarese heard that Father Francis was at Mannar, almost three thousand assembled for the deliverance. From Mannar he went on to Negapatan, and was surprised that the assembled Portuguese navy did not attack the kingdom of Jafnapatan, because the king had seized a rich cargo, Portuguese cargo vessel from Pegu. They taught that it was not a good time to declare war against the Prince of Jafnapatan because they would suffer irreversible loss. All hopes lost, Francis wanted to return to Travancore. However, he decided to take a pilgrimage to Mylapore, close to the tomb of St. Thomas the Apostle.

Pilgrimage to Mylapore

THE TOMB OF ST. THOMAS

MY LORD AND MY GOD

The tomb of St. Thomas

Francis took the journey by land through rough and difficult ways and within few days, arrived at Mylapore, present-day Tamil Nadu. On arrival he was welcomed by the Vicar who offered him his house which was adjacent to the church with the relics of St. Thomas. Francis took the opportunity to pray in the sacred shrine. While engaged in his devotions he wrote to two of his friends in Goa, Paul de Camerino, and James Borba: " I hope that God will confer many favours on me during this voyage since through His infinite goodness, I have learned with so much joy that it is his Holy Will that I should go to those kingdoms of Macassar, where so many Christians have lately been mad. I am so determined on executing what our Lord has revealed to me: that if I should be wanting on my part, I would act in direct opposition to His orders and render myself unworthy of this favour, both in this life and in the next. If I cannot this year find any Portuguese vessel bound for Moluccas, I will embark on any ship, whether it belongs to the pagans or the Saracens. I place so much confidence in God, for whose sake I undertake this voyage, that if there should pass this way a little bark of Moluccas I would unhesitatingly go on it. All my hope is in God; and I conjure you, by His love, always to remember, in your prayers, so great a sinner as I am." The reason for Francis' coming to Mylapore was to fulfill the direction from heaven.

At Mylapore, there was a Portuguese gentleman, who was living a scandalous and sacrilegious life with many beautiful slaves. Francis visited him during dinner time. The gentleman was annoyed but politely gave respect to the Father. Francis did not speak anything about the scandalous gentlemen and his way of life but left in silence. The silence of Francis spoke within the gentleman's heart. He anxiously sought out Francis, and falling down before him said, "Your silence has spoken powerfully to my heart. I have not enjoyed a moment's repose since you left me. If my everlasting doom be not already determined, I put myself into your hands. Do with me Father what you may judge necessary for the salvation of my Soul." Francis embraced him with tenderness and assured him of the mercies of the Lord for his repentance.

There was a merchant from Mylapore who was about to embark on a ship to Malacca. He went to meet Francis and to take his blessings for the safe journey. On receiving the blessing he asked a little token from him but Francis was very poor and could not give him anything, However, he took the beads from his neck and gave it to the merchant saying, "These beads will not be useless to you, provided you put your confidence in the Virgin Mary."

The merchant embarked on the ship and when they crossed the gulf, between Mylapore and Malacca, a storm suddenly arose and the vessel dashed against the rocks and opened. Most of the crew along with passengers were drowned. Some of them climbed on the rocks; along with them was the merchant who was full of confidence that he will not drown and kept faith in the beads. He was saved from drowning.

Francis stayed at Mylapore for almost four months, waiting for the ship, determined to take any ship. Through the messenger from the Governor of Goa, Francis learnt that a ship of the Portuguese King was leaving from the port of Mylapore for Malacca in the month of August 1545. There was also a letter from the Governor to the captain of the ship to give all the assistance for Francis to reach Malacca.

When the ship was about to sail to Malacca, present-day Malaysia, the vicar of Mylapore church gave Francis a token of appreciation for his tireless work for the parish. The token was a piece of the relic of St. Thomas which Francis kept in a small copper box and wore around his neck.

St. Francis Xavier Preaching by Carlone, Gesu, Rome

Francis in the Moluccas

The ship arrived at Malacca on the 25 September 1545. When Francis disembarked; he at once went to visit the governor of the town to inform him about his intention to go to Macassar. But the governor informed him that some holy priests were sent there and he was awaiting their response. Till then he advised him to stay at Malacca. Francis agreed, and as usual started visiting the hospital, and preaching.

He began his public instructions and translated the prayers into the Malaccan language as he had done in Goa. He went on the streets with a bell in his hand and started preaching. He learnt the Malaya tongue and soon translated a short catechism which he had composed at the Fishery Coast. With the help of this book he started teaching the Muslims and the Jews.

There was a youth, Antonio Fernandez, about fifteen years old who was sick. His mother tried all the natural remedies including superstition without success when a Christian woman told her to call Francis. When he arrived at the house of the dying youth, he presented the crucifix to him and read aloud the passion of Our Lord. He then placed his own reliquary about the neck of the sick person and sprinkled holy water. He told the father

of the youth to bring him to the church of Our Lady of the Mount. While he was celebrating the mass the next morning, the youth came to him, perfectly restored to health.

When Francis was a short distance from the city, a young woman had died at Malacca, and her mother sought for Francis. She met Francis, fell at his feet and said to him as Martha had said to Christ, "If you were there my daughter could have not died".

Francis was pleased with the faith of the woman, raised his eyes to God, prayed silently, and said to the woman: "Go; your daughter lives".

The woman was hesitant and replied "Three days have passed since she is buried".

"It is no matter", Francis said. "Open the grave and you will find her living."

She ran towards the church, opened the tomb and found her daughter living.

Francis waited for almost three months but there was no news from Macassar and no ship came from that island. On 1 January 1546, he embarked for Amboyna in a vessel which was bound for the island of Banda. During the voyage, he converted many Muslims and pagans, who were natives of India. From Amboyna, he waited for a vessel to bring him to Moluccas which was nearer to Macassar than Amboyna.

There was an island called Baranura where Francis mistakenly lost his crucifix in the sea. An eye-witness, Fausto Rodrigues, gives the account of the miraculous recovery of the crucifix.

"We were at sea," says Rodriguez, "Father Francis, John Rapose, and myself, when a violent storm arose, which alarmed all the crew. Xavier drew from his bosom a small crucifix, which he always carried with him, and leaned overboard intending to dip it into the sea but the crucifix dropped out of his hand, and sank out of sight. It was very manifest that this loss disturbed him considerably".

"We landed safe, however, next morning on the island of Baranura, although from the time when the crucifix was lost up to the moment of our landing, a space of twenty fours, we had been in continual danger. Francis and I were walking on shore, towards the town of Tamale. We had proceeded about five hundred paces, when we perceived a crab emerging from the sea, and bearing suspended in his

Miracle of Francis, by Nicolas Poussin

claws was the crucifix that had been lost. I saw the crab approach the Father and stop before him. He knelt down and took the crucifix; after which the crab returned to the sea. Xavier continued in the same posture for half an hour, pressing the crucifix to his breast, and affectionately kissing it. I joined him in returning thanks to God for so evident a miracle".

Francis returned to Amboyna and embarked for the Moluccas, present-day Indonesia, in a Portuguese vessel.

The Moluccas are tiny islands famous for spice. The main islands were Ternate, Tidor, Motir, Macian, and Bacian. These islands were discovered by the voyager Magallanes in 1511 and the Portuguese started their trade from the Ternate Island. Francis was in the vessel which was known as *caracores* and another similar ship carried Juna Galvan, Both sailed together from Amboyna and kept company as they headed to the port of Ternate. In the middle of gulf, a violent storm put them apart and through the dangers of the storm the *caracores* arrived at the port of Ternate.

On his arrival, Francis was preaching when he suddenly paused and prayed, "Pray for the soul of Juna Galvan, who has been drowned in the gulf." Some of the people who were present and awaiting the arrival of Juna Galvan were eager to know the truth: after ten or twelve days a ship arrived for Amboyna and confirmed his death.

Francis then went to the Isle del Moro and thereafter returned to Moluccas intending to sail to Goa, hoping to bring some missionaries from Goa for the new churches he had established in the islands. At the Ternate Island he resided near the chapel of "Our Lady of the Port" for three months and occupied himself in the tribunal of penance. During his stay Francis composed and gave many instructions in the Malaya language.

He set sail for Malacca twenty days after his arrival at Amboyna. Francis on reaching Malacca, he found three missionaries of the society who were going to the Moluccas in obedience to his directions; these were John Beyra, Nugnez Ribera, priest, and Nicholas Nugnez. Mansilla was not with them and preferred to stay back and labour where he was. Francis expelled him from the Society for his disobedience and sent the missionaries to Moluccas.

Francis met a nobleman from Kagoshima by name Anjiro. Anjiro had heard about Francis in 1545 and had travelled from Kagoshima to Malacca to meet Francis.

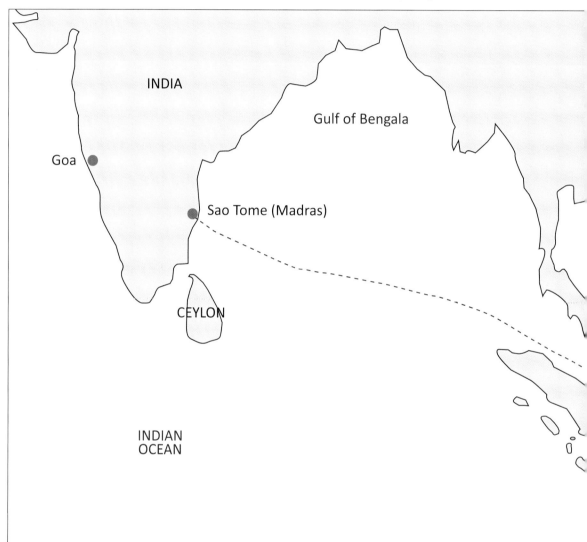

o the Moluccas

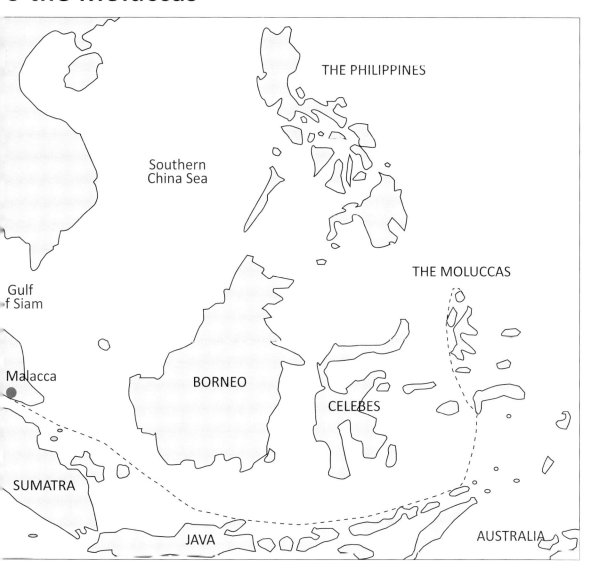

THE PHILIPPINES

Southern
China Sea

THE MOLUCCAS

Gulf
f Siam

Malacca

BORNEO

CELEBES

SUMATRA

JAVA

AUSTRALIA

Map of Small Islands in the Moluccas

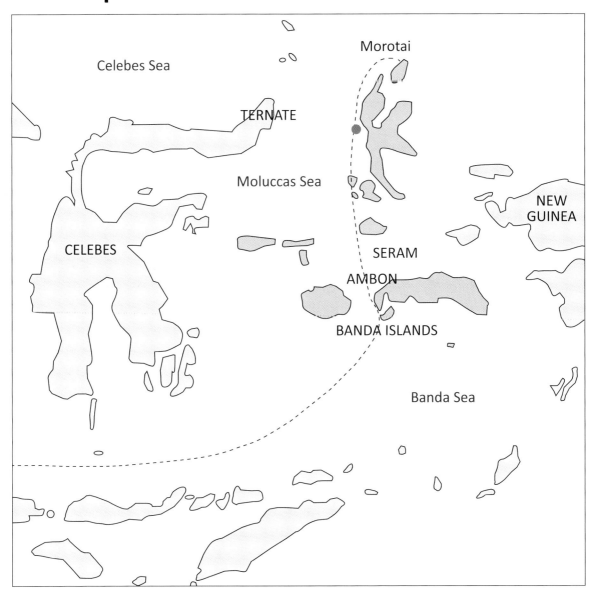

Celebes Sea

Morotai

TERNATE

Moluccas Sea

NEW GUINEA

CELEBES

SERAM

AMBON

BANDA ISLANDS

Banda Sea

Voyage to Japan

Francis returned to India in January 1548 and for the next fifteen months was occupied with various journeys and administrative measures in India. Francis sailed to Cochin, leaving Goa on 15 April 1549 with the intention of going to Japan. He chose as his companions: Fr. Cosmas de Torres, Brother Juan Fernandez, both of them Spaniards; Anjiro who was baptised in Goa as Paul de Sainte Foi and two of his attendants, Juan and Antonio. From Cochin they boarded the vessel for Malacca on 31 May.

At Malacca there was no Portuguese vessel to sail for Japan, therefore Francis resolved to go on a Chinese vessel which was going directly to Japan. Francis and his companions embarked on 29 June. After many events on board, the vessel was driven by the strong winds towards the coast of Japan. On 15 August 1549, they landed at Kagoshima, the birthplace of Paul de Sainte Foi.

Japanese painting of St. Francis Xavier

Francis and his companions went to pay their homage to the King of Saxuma. Paul de Sainte Foi who knew the King was welcomed with great pleasure as the king was of the opinion that Paul was dead. The prince was curious and started inquiring about India and the character of the people and the Portuguese. Paul explained in detail and took the opportunity to speak about Christianity which the Portuguese had introduced.

Paul showed the King a picture of the Virgin with child Jesus in her arms, which Francis had given him. He was astonished and respectfully knelt down in honour of the picture. He ordered that the picture be shown to the Queen. She was equally amazed and asked many questions concerning the Blessed Virgin and the Child Jesus. She was completely enthralled and wanted to copy the picture. Francis

Map Showing the Voyage from Malacca to Japan

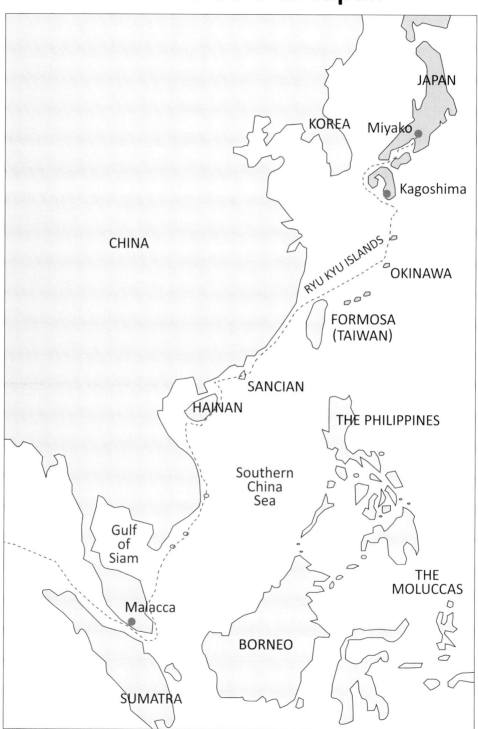

JAPAN

KOREA

Miyako

Kagoshima

CHINA

RYU KYU ISLANDS

OKINAWA

FORMOSA
(TAIWAN)

SANCIAN

HAINAN

THE PHILIPPINES

Southern
China
Sea

Gulf
of
Siam

THE
MOLUCCAS

Malacca

BORNEO

SUMATRA

Map of Japan Where Francis Preached

was overjoyed with the event and wanted to preach in the language of the country.

Though Francis was familiar with the language through the three Japanese converts, it was not enough for him to preach the Gospel. So he started learning Japanese grammar. While Francis was learning the language, Paul de Sainte Foi, instructed his family. His mother, wife and daughter took baptism at the hands of Francis. Within forty days Francis managed to learn the language and translated the "Apostles' Creed", but could not preach as the laws in Japan were rigid: he could not do anything without the prior permission of the King.

Francis with the help of Paul took an audience with the King as Francis was well known to the court since Paul had already talked about him. The King gave permission to Francis and cautioned him to be careful: "If your faith be true, the demons will be sure to attack you, and exert all their malice against you". The king also published an edict which permitted all to embrace Christianity if they desired.

With the favours granted by the King, Francis started proclaiming the Gospel to the people of Kagoshima and performed many miracles.

There was a woman who heard about Francis and the miracles he performed in India and approached him with her child who was deformed by unnatural tumors, Francis took the child in his arms and said "God Bless Thee." and the child was restored to perfect health.

There was a young lady, who was dead, and her father could not be consoled. Some converts told him to meet Francis; he took courage, went to meet him, fell at his feet, and started pleading him to restore his beloved daughter. Francis along with his companion prayed to God and said, "Go, your daughter liveth". But the man was dissatisfied as he was expecting Francis to come over to his house. On his way back, servants came running towards him and proclaimed "Your daughter is alive". The father immediately brought the daughter to Francis and Fernandez and she cried "Behold my deliverers". Everyone was amazed at the power of the Christian Faith.

Francis and his companions thereafter voyaged by sea and arrived at the Port of Firando. The king of Firando heard about Francis from the king of Kagoshima and knew about Father Francis. The King gave permission to the three missionaries to publish the law of Jesus Christ in his kingdom and the people flocked in large

Painting of St. Francis Xavier baptising the Japanese

Matthew and Bernard, left for Meaco and landed there in February 1551, but since they could not achieve much there, they decided to go to Yamaguchi. Here he wanted an audience with the Emperor and waited in front of the Palace for almost eleven days but the attire of Francis and his companions was not impressive. As it was customary for the Japanese to judge the person on the dress code, his mission was a failure at Kyoto. He returned to Yamaguchi, desperate. Francis was well aware that his shabby appearance had made a negative impact on Japanese as they were of high rank.

After a few days of his arrival, the secretary Naito obtained necessary permission to meet the king. This time Francis approached the king as the ambassador of the Governor of Portuguese India. He was elegantly dressed with silk cassock and took with him gifts from India. He presented to the king the letters of the governor and the bishop of India, and requested him to give the permission to preach as it was the only motive of his Journey.

The King admired Francis and gave him the permission and a public edict. The king also gave them residence which was an old habitation of the Bonzas. Francis settled there and many people

number to hear the first sermon of Xavier. He made such an impression on the natives that within twenty days he baptised many.

In October 1550, Francis along with Fernndez and two Japanese Christians,

Portuguese ship to Japan

came to meet him. Francis preformed many miracles in Japan. Father Antonio Quadros, who went to Japan four years later wrote about it to Father Diego Moron the provincial of Portugal. "A Japannese informed me that he had witnessed three miracles performed by Francis in his country. One was the cure and restoration to speech of a palsied and dumb person. The others were the cure of two persons, one of whom was deaf, the other dumb. This man also told me that Father Xavier was esteemed by the Japanese as the most learned of the Europeans. He said that the other Fathers of the Society were not to be compared with him because they could only answer one person at a time, whereas Xavier, by a single word, answered ten or twelve questions."

"When I remarked that this might probably be accounted for, by supposing the questions to be somewhat similar, he assured me that such was not the case, but that they were on many different subjects. He added, in fine, that this was not a rare thing with him, but rather his ordinary practice."

Francis and his companion, Fernandez, started preaching publicly twice a day

St. Francis Xavier Church, Hirado Japan

without any opposition from the Bonzas. The monasteries of the Bonzas started decreasing and they abandoned their way of life and became converts. After preaching the Gospel to the Bonzas and performing many miracles, he intended to visit China.

Francis wanted to return to India to bring some missionaries to Japan. He had conversations with a Chinese merchant who was residing at Yamaguchi and thought that if the polished and intelligent Japanese could be brought to Christianity, then it would be easy to convert the Chinese. The Japanese were accustomed to say that they would not alter their religion until the Chinese had led the way. "Let him carry the gospel," said they, "to that vast and flourishing empire; and when he has gained it to Jesus Christ, then we may entertain the idea of adopting it."

There was a Portuguese vessel which was commanded by Edward de Gama and it arrived at the kingdom of Bungo. Francis heard about this vessel, which would return to India within a month and sent a Japanese convert by name of Mathew to Bungo. He submitted a letter requesting them to take him to India. The ship was docked at the port of Figen. Francis left for Bungo and on arrival he met the king of Bungo and stayed till he got the news of the departure of the Vessel.

On 20 November 1551, Francis set sail. He had stayed for almost two years and four months in Japan.

St. Francis Xavier Church, Yahashi

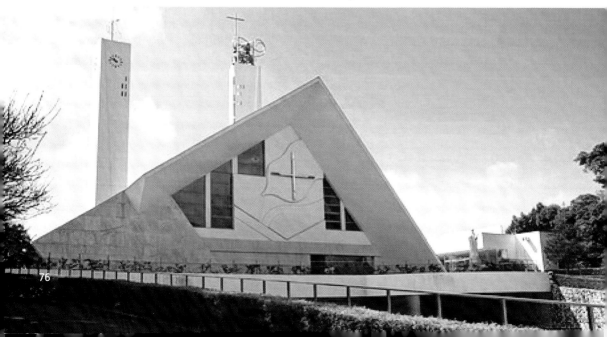

The Final Mission

Francis Celebrating Mass at St. Paul's college

Francis arrived at Goa in the beginning of February and soon visited the sick in the public hospitals and went to the college of St. Paul which belonged to the Society. He named Flemish Gaspar Berze as the Rector of St. Paul's College and also as Vice Provincial. He arranged the affairs of the society and accordingly sent Melchior Nugnez to Bazain, Gonsalvo Rodriguez to Cochin, John Lopez to Meliapore, and Louis Menez to the Fishery Coast. He then started preparing himself to procure an embassy to China.

The viceroy, Don Alphonso de Norogna, nominated James Pereyar as the ambassador and promised to give a large sum of money to procure presents for the Emperor. Elaborate arrangements were made for the voyage.

On 14 April 1552, Francis sailed from Goa and then from Cochin to Malacca. The journey from Goa to Malacca was not favourable as the ship Santiago was in danger of being wrecked more than once.

As soon he landed at Malacca, he started visiting the sick, accompanied by his companions; he went on the streets, hospitals and even made arrangements

Francis arrived at Cochin on 24 January 1552 and met the king of Madliver islands, who was a Muslim and against Christianity; he was forced to take asylum among the Portuguese. Francis spoke to the king and convinced him, and he was solemnly baptised. The prince was later brought to Goa and placed by the Portuguese in the college of St. Paul.

Voyage from Malacca to Sancian

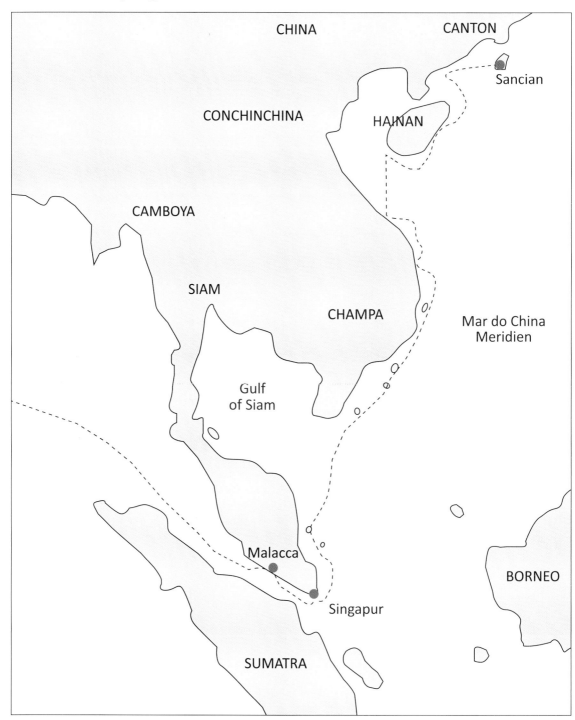

for the sick to be housed in the college of the Society as there was an epidemical disease raging.

There was a young man, named Francis Ciavus, the only son of a devout woman, who mistakenly endangered his life with one of his poisoned arrows and died. While the family and friends were engaged in burying him, Francis was passing by and heard the cry and lamentations of the disconsolate mother. Francis said, "Francis, in the name of Jesus Christ, arise" and the young man immediately arose, and was obliged to dedicate his life to God. He resolved to enter the Society.

When Francis was in Malacca, he met Dom Alvaro da Gama who was the son of Vasco da Gama, a Portuguese Commandant In Malacca, and requested him to obtain permission from the Chinese Emperor since he had decided to go to China, as official representative of the Portuguese Government. Francis was supposed to go as an Apostolic Nuncio and Diogo Pereira as the Ambassador. No one knew that Francis was officially appointed as Apostolic Nuncio, except the Bishop of Goa who kept this secret for ten years.

When Dom Alvaro de Athaide da Gama learnt that Diogo Pereia, a merchant, was chosen as the Ambassador to the Emperor of China, he was furious and refused to allow the ship and its owner to sail. Francis was disheartened and expressed his feelings to his friend James Pereyar: "Since the greatness of my sins has been the cause why God Almighty would not make use of us for the embassy to China, I charge my own conscience with all the fault. My offences have ruined your fortune, and caused you to lose all the expense of the embassy to China; and yet I declare before God that I love him and you also. Had not my intentions been right, I would have been yet more afflicted than I am. I ask you as a favour not to visit me; lest the condition to which you are reduced, should give me additional pain, and thus your sorrow only tend to increase mine. I hope, however, that this disappointment will turn to your advantage, as I have no doubt but that the king will reward your zeal, and I have requested him to do so by letters. As for the governor, who has broken up our plans, I have no further communication with him. May God forgive him. I pity him, and deplore his condition for he will be soon punished and that much more severely than he imagines."

Francis dropped the plan to go as the Pope's legate but he determined to go to China and embarked on the ship "Santa Cruz", which was going to Sancian. He

St. Francis Xavier, Lorenzo de Caro

Painting, Bom Jesus Basilica, miracle of water

anticipated that going to China was risky; so he planned to go alone and took along with him Antonio de Santa Fe, a Chinese brother of the society. The ship carried about five hundred persons which included the crew and the passengers. During the voyage the ship suddenly became motionless because there was no wind and remained steady for almost fourteen days as if it was anchored. Many died for want of water, and many were sick. They requested Francis to pray for water or for a favourable wind. Francis told the voyagers to pray with confidence in Jesus Christ and to recite the litany on their knees before a large crucifix. He then went to his cabin, took a child along with him, took the sea water and asked the child to taste the water. He asked her whether the water was salty or fresh. The child answered that it was salty. He made the sign of the cross over the water and gave it to taste and they found it to be fresh water. Witnessing the miracle, many fell at his feet and asked for baptism.

During course of the voyage, a little child of five years accidently fell into the sea. Her father was not converted in spite of the miracle of the water he had seen. The father was inconsolable for the loss of his child. Francis heard about this and approached him and said, "If God were to restore the child to you, would you become a sincere Christian?" He agreed, and after three days the child was discovered on the hatches. Seeing this miracle, the entire family embraced the faith, and the child took the name of Francis.

The ship passed from Cincheo to Sancian, a small Island, after a voyage of twenty-three days from Malacca. The vessel "Santa Cruz" anchored before this island. Since the Chinese were not permitting the strangers to visit their country, the Portuguese carried on their trade in this Island.

From the time he landed on this island, he was waiting in hope to get a passage to the mainland. The Portuguese were happy because Francis was at Sancian. When they came to know that his intention was to go to China, they started protesting as the Mandarins were cruel to strangers, and they did not want Francis to take the risk of going to China. Nothing could convince Francis as his only motto was to go to China. There was no one to transport Francis to China because the penalty for violation of the law was death.

A Chinese merchant offered to take Francis to the province of Canton if he was paid well. Though he agreed with the merchant he was not sure whether the merchant would fulfil the promise.In one of his letters, he writes: "I perceive two dangers almost inevitable in this affair. There is a danger that the idolatrous merchant, when he has received my money, may throw me overboard, or abandon me on some desert isle; and in the second place, it is to be feared that the governor of Canton may discharge his fury on my head, and by putting me to a cruel death, or consigning me to perpetual imprisonment, make me an example to all foreigners. But in case I follow the voice that calls me, and obey the Lord, I esteem life and liberty as nothing."

Francis fell sick with violent fever which lasted for fifteen days and recovered. But on 20 November, Francis was ill with

The suffering of Francis, by Baciccia

The death of Francis, by Gaetano Lapes

fever again. Meanwhile the mandarins at Canton had stopped the supplies of food on which the sojourner at Sancian depended. The merchant who had taken the reward to take Francis to Canton did not turn up. The interpreter on whom Francis was depending also gave up the plan because his courage failed him. There was no hope remaining to go to China. Francis was exhausted with fever and at this moment he thought of nothing other than heavenly things.

When he was first attacked by fever he was taken on board the *Santa Cruz* which was a substitute for a Hospital, but the motion of the ship made it difficult to concentrate on God, and he requested to be taken ashore. George Alvarez could not see Francis lying on the ground, in the open air. So took him to his own hut, which gave him shelter from cold, wind and rain. George thought it would be better to bleed the patient and the operation was done twice by an inexperienced man. Francis fainted with the pain.

Francis suffered so much that he could not eat even a few almonds which the captain of the ship sent him as a present. He went on suffering for a week. The disease continued to increase, and he became weaker day by day. Sometimes he would raise his eyes to heaven, and sometimes he would fix his eyes on his crucifix. On 28 November, he became seriously ill and he spoke nothing but of God and of his entrance into China.

He however lost his speech for three days and became weaker; but on Wednesday he regained it. He begged that the vestments and sacred vessels which he had used for mass, as well his manuscript of the Christian doctrine in Chinese letters and the rest to be taken to the ship. Antonio de Santa Fe, the Chinese, and Cristoval were the only attendants. Francis spoke a good deal in ejaculations in Latin, Antonio recorded that he frequently repeated these words '*O Sanctissima Trinitas*', '*Jesu Fili David miserere mei,*' and '*Monstra te esse matrem*'. The fever persisted; he grew weaker and weaker.

On the second of December 1552, about two in the afternoon, he fixed his eyes lovingly upon his crucifix, his face lit up with joy, sweet tears poured from his eyes, and he breathed his last, repeating the words of the *Te Deum*: "*In te Domine speravi, non confundar in æternum!*" (In thee, O Lord! have I hoped, I shall not be confounded for ever.)

At the time of his death he was forty six years old.

The Incorruptible Body of the Saint

The first tomb of St. Francis Xavier at Sancian Island

On hearing of the death of Francis, some of the Portuguese belonging to the ship came to see the corpse. There was no funeral ceremony. Only four persons assisted: Antonio de Santa Fe, Francis d' Aghiar and two others. They took off his cassock, which was torn is several places and divided it among themselves as a relic of the departed saint. George Alvares had a coffin made, in which the body was placed, and filled it with quick lime in order that the flesh might be consumed so that the bones could be taken to India. On the grave they planted a wooden cross and mounted two stones one at the head and other at the feet.

Days passed, and in the middle of February the ship was about to sail to Malacca. Antonio, the Chinese, asked the captain to examine the corpus so that the bones of Francis could be taken to India. The coffin was opened and the lime was removed. The body was found to be entirely fresh and soft, the veins full of blood, even the vestments were not hurt by the lime. The Portuguese examined the body and cut off a small piece from the left knee: they found blood flowing freely.

The news was conveyed to the captain and immediately the Portuguese who had abandoned Francis when he was sick came to venerate him, weeping and begging pardon for their neglect. Then the coffin along with the body was taken on board *Santa Cruz* and the ship sailed for Malacca and reached on 22 March 1553.

At Malacca, there was no one of the Society to receive them. Some priests were sent on board by the Vicar to take possession of the body. It was examined and its preservation was testified. The next day a solemn procession was organised and the body was carried to the Church of Our Lady del Mont. People flocked to see the incorruptible body of Francis and paid their respects with torched candles. The Plague which affected Malacca ceased suddenly.

The body of Francis was laid to rest for the second time in the doorway leading to the sacristy, covered with earth but without the coffin. As the grave was too short while burying, the shoulder was wounded and blood flowed.

When Joam Beira arrived at Malacca with two of the companions from Moluccas, he wanted to see the body which was laid to rest. Secretly, Diego Pereira and some other devout friends opened the grave of Francis and found it to be in fresh and perfect condition, the cloth which was spread over the face was blood stained. Diego Pereira made a magnificent coffin and the body was laid, resting on a cushion and covered with a coverlet of gold cloth.

The coffin was later transported in 1553 on board an old unworthy vessel, which arrived in January at Cochin where the body was venerated by a large crowd. When the news of the arrival of the body to India was conveyed to Goa, the authorities in Goa did not want the ship to arrive during the Holy Week; therefore, Fr. Nunes Barreto, who had succeeded Xavier in the office as the Provincial of the Jesuits, obtained permission from the Viceroy to send a fast sailing vessel in order to bring the body before the Holy Week. The Viceroy immediately arranged a fast sailing vessel and sent the superior of the college of St. Paul, Barreto, along with two religious to escort the body to Goa.

The second Tomb of St. Francis Xavier at Malacca

This was not the only intention of Barreto. He was a Doubting Thomas. Everyone around Goa was talking about the incorruptible body of Francis but Barreto doubted: "Unless I set my eyes upon that body and pass my hand over it, I will not believe". He met the old ship at Bhatkal in North Kanara, and along with Manuel Teixeira, entered the cabin where the body was laid and inspected. In a letter to Ignatius in Rome dated 3 December 1554, he wrote: "I saw and studied with my eyes and handled it with my hands and I who had been incredulous till then cried in astonishment. He has made his wonderful works to be remembered, being a merciful and gracious Lord."

The body of Francis reached the harbour of Goa on the Thursday, 15 March during Passion Week, and anchored opposite the Church of Our Lady at Ribandar. On 16 March 1554 six barks, magnificently adorned, carrying the chief of Portuguese nobility, came to Ribandar followed by twelve more barks with bands of instruments and vocal music. They were lined up in two divisions and in midst of these, the galley which bore the sacred body of Francis passed. All of Goa and its inhabitants gathered on the shore awaiting the arrival of the body of their beloved Father.

On the quay was the Viceroy with his Court, council and the religious community of the college. The orphans carried a large crucifix for it was Passion Week and the procession went through the street impressively up to the College of St. Paul. The sacred body arrived into the church and was placed near the High Altar and a solemn Mass with a concert of voices and instruments created a great feast. Thereafter, the coffin was opened for inspection by the Viceroy and other dignitaries, civil and ecclesiastical.

The first examination of the body of St. Francis took place as soon as it arrived in Goa from Malacca, when the Viceroy Dom Affonso de Noronha ordered an official medical examination of the Body. Doctor Cosmas Saraiva, his personal physician, and Dr. Ambrosio Rebeiro, the Vicar-General, examined the Body.

The Examinations

Dr. Cosmas Saraiva gives the account of the examination: "I felt and pressed all the members of the body with my finger, but paid special attention to the abdominal region and made certain that the intestines were in their natural position. There had been no embalming of any kind nor had any artificial preservative agents been used. I observed a wound in the left side near the heart and asked

Painting, voyage of the Incorruptible Body of St. Francis Xavier to Goa

two of the Society, who were with me to put their fingers into it. When they withdrew them, they were covered with blood which I smelt and found absolutely untainted. The limbs and other parts of the body were entire and clothed in their flesh in such a way that, according to the laws of medicine, they could not possibly have been so preserved by any natural or artificial means, seeing that Father Francis had been dead for a year and a half and buried for a year."

This was reinforced by the account of the examination of the body by Dr. Ambrosio Rebeiro: "I felt the body with my own hands from the feet up the knees and about all the other parts of the body. I certify that in all these parts the flesh was entire, covered with its natural skin and humidity without any corruption. On the left leg a little above the knee on the exterior there is a little cut or wound, a finger length, which looked like a hit. All round the wound there oozed out a streak of blood gone black. And much above it on the left side near the heart there is a small hole which looked like a hit. Through it, I inserted my fingers deep as I could and found it hollow. Only inside I felt some small bits which seemed to me like pieces of intestines dried up due to the long times the body lay in the grave. But I smelt no corruption although I put my face quite close to the body. The head rested on a small Chinese damask pillow leaving on it below the neck something like a stain of blood similar to that on the leg, faded in colour and turned black."

The Dissections of the Body

As mentioned the first mutilation took place at Sancian when a piece of skin and muscle was cut from the body after exhumation by the captain of the ship. During the first exposition in 16-18 March 1554, on arrival in Goa an emotional Portuguese noblewoman, Isabel Caron, bit off the last toe of the right foot to keep it as a relic and another person took a piece of flesh.

On 3 November 1614 by order and devotion of the Superior General of the Society of Jesus, Claudio Aquaviva, the entire right upper limb was disarticulated: the forearm with shrunken hand and fingers was sent to Rome and the remaining parts distributed as relics; the upper arm was then sent to Japan; the shoulder blade was divided into three parts, one for each College of Cochin, Malacca and Macau.

Again in 1620 or sometime later, with the request of another Superior, Veteleschi, the real dissection was performed by eleven expert doctors and the internal

Torriani, St. Francis Xavier, Lucerne

Relic of the arm of St. Francis Xavier in the Church of Gesu, Rome

organs were removed and put into a heap for distribution as relics.

By 1659 the sacred relics were scattered all over the world.

In 1681 the Provincial Fernao Queiros, fearing the dissected body might crumble into dust, asked the Superior General to order not to open the coffin. The request was then renewed by Provincial Gaspar Afonso and according to these requests, the Superior General, M.A. Tamburini, ordered that the body be kept in a lead coffin so that it could not be opened. The order was complied with by Provincial M. Saraiva.

In 1708, Francis de Sousa, as Prefect of the Professed House, asked the same Superior for authorisation to throw into "the bottom of the Ocean" the keys of the outer silver blades so that not even through the crystal could anyone observe the relics.

On 2 April 1755, the King of Portugal ordered that, without his permission it should not be opened under any circumstances or in favour of any person, however great. Ten years later, the same sovereign ordered that the coffin should have three different keys and named the key holders.

Francis Xavier the Saint

Father Francis Xavier was beatified on 25 October 1619 by Pope Paul V and canonised on 12 March 1622 by Pope Gregory XV. St. Ignatius Loyola was also canonised on the same day.

The sacred body of St. Francis Xavier was incorrupt for over 150 years and was examined and dissected several times.

The body is now shrunken in size, and it is no longer intact, but the fact remains that corruption, however, has never touched it.

The coffin with three keys, Bom Jesus Basilica

St. Francis Xavier, by Miguel Cabrera

The Basilica of Bom Jesus

The Professed House of Bom Jesus was erected by the Jesuits in 1585 and it was the third house of the Society in the city. The original name of the house was Jesus. The residential house was extended and the Jesuits settled in it on 12 January 1586, the entire building of the Professed House was completed in 1589. The present Professed House is only a part of the original structure, some of its long corridors and spacious apartments have disappeared with time and during the flames of fire in 1663 and then again in 1783. Before canonisation in 1622, the Relic of Francis Xavier was kept on the third floor.

Attached to the Professed House is the Minor Basilica of Bom Jesus wherein lies the sacred Relic of St. Francis Xavier. The foundation stone for the Basilica was laid on 24 November 1594, and it was consecrated by the Archbishop of Goa, D. Aleixo de Meneses.

The façade is facing towards the west and it is a combination of Doric, Corinthian and Composite styles. It is built of black granite adorned with graceful pillars, reliefs and carvings.

As the storey diminishes from the bottom to its height, so the decorations increase in complexity, until the pediment is reached which is artistically and richly carved, displaying the medallion of the coats of arms of the Society.

The Basilica is built of red laterite stones and most of the decorations in the façade including columns are of black granites.

The interior of the Basilica is built in Mosaico-Corinthian style and is remarkable for its charming simplicity. The ceiling is of wood with intricately carved brackets. The Basilica is of a single nave but it is spacious and has underneath it, the choir and no side aisles.

The pillars which support the choir bears two inscriptions in Latin and Portuguese, which inform when the construction of the church of Jesus commenced. At the entrance on either side, there are altars on the northern side that contain a statue of St. Francis Xavier behind which there is an old baptismal font. Opposite to it the altar contains the statue of St. Anthony.

In the middle of the nave towards the right, there is a richly carved pulpit which depicts the four gospel writers; opposite to the pulpit there is a cenotaph of bronze supported by two lions that contains the mortal remains of the founder of the Church, Dom Jeronimo Mascarenhas.

Façade of Bom Jesus Basilica

Main altar of Bom Jesus Basilica

The main altar is completely Baroque in style, with twisted columns supporting two angels, and in the middle is the statue of St. Ignatius Loyola, dressed in priestly vestments and he is slightly raised in his customary pose. The whole altar is covered in pure gold. The statue of Child Jesus is exposed on the pedestal of that of St. Ignatius and on the top is the sculpture of the Blessed Trinity, which Ignatius contemplates through the medallion containing the Greek letters I.H.S.

The lateral altars are dedicated to Our Lady of Mercy and to St. Michael. The transept ends on either side with the chapel on the left of the Most Blessed Sacrament and on the right, the chapel of St. Francis Xavier. Both these chapels are vaulted like the main chapel.

The Chapel of the Blessed Sacrament is dedicated to St. Francis of Borja. On this Altar was kept from 1624 the Relic of the body of St. Francis Xavier for 35 years. In the year 1659 the Relic was then transferred to the present site opposite to the chapel in the Mausoleum.

Richly carved Pulpit, Bom Jesus Basilica

The Chapel of St. Francis Xavier

The Chapel has doors on four sides and its roof is rib-vaulted with paintings in each section. This Chapel was built specially in the year 1655, in order to place the Relic there once for all. The Chapel, though situated in a narrow

Mausoleum, Chapel of St. Francis Xavier

St. Francis Xavier baptising the natives of Moluccas

and dark space, without conditions for the rich tomb to be duly contemplated, is interiorly decorated with paintings and gildings. The walls are adorned with 29 picture frames representing the life and miracles of the glorious Apostle of the East.

The mausoleum is about six meters in height from the base to the cross. It is three meters in length and two and a half in width, is made of three parts besides the silver coffin. The tomb is full of marbles of various colours. It is said that the mausoleum was an offer from the Great Duke Cosmas III (1670-1723), of Toscana, in return, for the pillow on which the head of the Saint reposed for many years after his death.

The first part of the mausoleum is made of four altars forming an urn, one on each side of the tomb. The whole urn is made of red jasper radiating bright light. With decoration *tarjas* as well as the eight *cherubims* in the four corners, made of pure alabaster.

In the center of the frontal of each of the altars, there is an emblem in high relief. Thus the frontal of the northern side shows the Sun with two concentric radiating circles; that of the southern side, a heart exhaling flames between two radiating circles; that of the western side, a clouded sky emanating rays and finally that of the head a book and various crosses coming down upon it.

The second part forms a regular quadrangle, of jasper with white, black and grey spots, with outshining frieze of yellow marble with white and black veils. On the four sides of the parallelepiped, four blades of bronze form *panneaux* panels in high relief, representing four episodes of the life of the Saint. It also contains large conspicuous sprays of lilies on either side of the two bronze plates, on the longer sides of the monument.

The panel of the face turned towards the church shows St. Francis preaching to the wild men of Moluccas. At the top of the panel, a medallion of bronze, depicting the rising sun, is supported by two big angels of alabaster, and is finished with a ribbon also of bronze, with a legend *Mox inimica fugat* (He drives away at once all hostilities).

Persecuting of St. Francis Xavier

Front view of the Mausoleum

The panel on the side of the head shows the Apostle barefooted, with surplice and stole, the Cross in the left hand, baptising the people of the Moluccas. A medallion represents the sun in its zenith and a ribbon is held by two angles with legend: *ut vitam habeant* (That they may have life) which completes the panel.

The panel on the south shows the Saint trying to cross a river on a wooden plank in order to run away for the fury of the islanders of Moro who were persecuting him with arrows and stones. In the medallion that tops the panel one can see a lion in the midst of a furious tempest with a symbolic legend: *Nihil horum vereor* (I fear none of these).

The final panel on the side of the foot-rest represents the death of the saint, on the seashore of Sancian, almost overlooking China that the saint wanted to evangelize, embracing a crucifix and laid in a hut of the Portuguese George Alvares, dying in the arms of his disciples, Antonio and Christovao, with the assistance the legend: *Major in Occasu* (Greater is setting).

The third part of the Mausoleum is made up of a marble balustrade of purple colour with white spots. The Friezes of the four columns of the angels are made of black marble and of a white bright colour. The squares that serve as a foundation are made of yellow stones of silicon type.

On this balustrade is placed the coffin with the precious Relic of the Saint. All along one finds the coffin garnished in laced silver on background red velvet. This silver casket is a masterpiece in its own right made by Indian artists. On the four sides of the coffin, there exist in two rows, thirty two blades of silver with the number of phases and miracles of the saint. A cross made of silver, tops the coffin, on whose pedestal one can see two angels with emblems in their hands; the one on the side of the head has in his hand an inflamed heart, and that on the side of the feet with the following legend: *Satis est, Domine satis est*. "Enough, Lord enough" expression that the saint uttered once in an ecstasy of love.

Inside the coffin is the safe in which lies the Relic of the Saint dressed in vestments embroidered in gold and decorated with pearls, offered by the Queen of Portugal, D. Maria Sofia. On the side of the feet is the gold medallion

offered by Dom Pedro II. And on the right side, the baton encrusted in gold and 194 emeralds.

In 1922 the coat of arms was fixed on the tomb which constitutes the coat of arms of the family of the Saint: Jassos, Atondos, Azphilquetas and Xavier the following inscription being on the reverse "In commemoration of the 3rd Centenary of canonization of St. Francisco Xavier".

Silver Coffin of the Saint

Expositions of the Sacred Relic

Relic of St. Francis Xavier

In 1744, the newly appointed Viceroy, Pedro Minguel, and Archbishop Frey Lorenzo were very eager to see the Relic and took the permission of the King of Portugal to open the casket. They had also brought some new vestments given by the Queen. On 11 December 1774 the casket was opened and the body was taken out and the new vestments put. The old and the new Viceroys and Metropolitans were able to view the Relic.

In the year 1759, the Society of Jesus was suppressed in the lands which they controlled and the Church of Bom Jesus along with body of St. Francis Xavier came under the control of the Archdiocese of Goa. From then onwards the body was exposed for the veneration of all the devotees at irregular intervals and during special occasions.

I Exposition: 10 to 12 February 1782

Rumours had spread among the people of Goa that the Jesuits had taken away the sacred relic of St. Francis Xavier when they were expelled from Goa, and arrested as criminals and prisoners. To reassure the

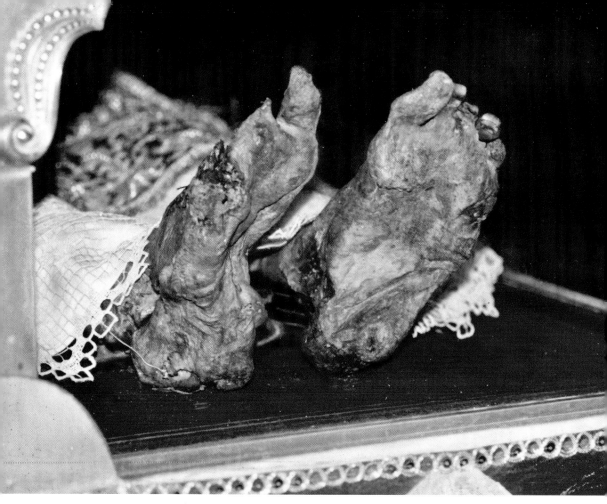

Photo of the Relics of the legs of St. Francis Xavier

public that the sacred Relic was still in Goa, the civil and ecclesiastical authorities decided to hold a short exposition.

On 1 January, the Relic was inspected and they found that the body was vested in sacerdotal robes, the head intact, with enough hair, the skull was visible, the face shrunken but covered with skin, the ears intact and all the teeth, except a missing one, visible; the left arm and hand was shrunk but covered with skin; the rest of the body entire but without intestines.

The Archbishop ascertained, by passing his hand below the vestments, that the thighs and feet had shrunk, but still covered with skin, the veins were visible; the toes still had their nails, though one of them was missing. So the authorities were satisfied that the relic could be exposed for public veneration.

II Exposition: 3 December 1859 to 8 January 1860

The Governor General of Goa, Daman and Diu, took permission of the King of

Portugal for an Exposition of St. Francis Xavier and was held for 37 days after examining the body. More than 2, 00,000 pilgrim venerated and eight people were cured from their illness during this Exposition.

III Exposition: 3 December 1878 to 6 January 1879

This Exposition was held under the Archbishop Primate of the Indies, D. Ayres de Ornelas de Vasconcelos, and it was attended by twelve bishops and three hundred priests; more that 3,00,000 people venerated the sacred Relic of St. Francis Xavier.

IV Exposition: 3 December 1890 to 1 January 1891

The Exposition was arranged by Archbishop-Patriarch of Goa, Dom Antonio Sebastiao Valente. More than 30,000 pilgrims attended the first day. The opening day ceremony was attended by Archbishop Goethals of Calcutta, Bishops Gasnier of Dacca,

Exposition photo of the relics St. Francis Xavier, 1964-65

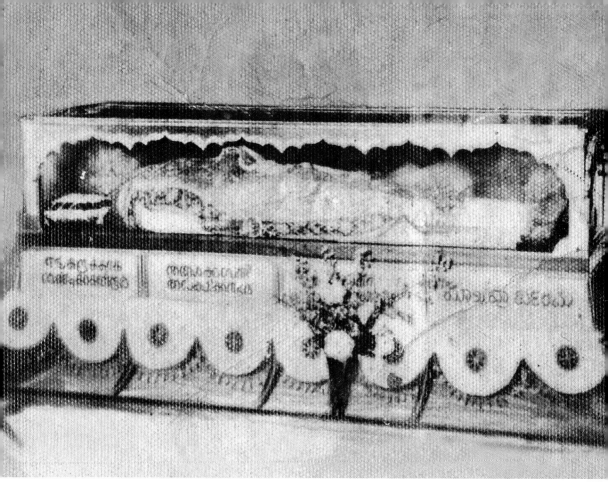

Exposition photo of the relics of St. Francis Xavier, 1974-75

Caprotti of Hyderabad and Beider-Linden from Poona, the Bishops of Cochin and Mylapore and some Vicar-Generals. 1,71,000 persons kissed the Relic of St. Francis Xavier.

V Exposition: 7 to 10 December 1900

The motive of holding a short Exposition was that the Eucharistic Congress was held in Goa, in the Sacristy of the Bom Jesus Basilica in Goa. After the Congress, the Archbishop-Partiarch, D. Sebastiao Valente, organised the Exposition of the Relic.

VI Exposition: 26 November to 28 December 1910

This Exposition was in commemoration of the second and definitive occupation of Goa by Affonso de Albuquerque on 25 November 1510. 5,00,000 people venerated the sacred Relic of St. Francis Xavier and many miracles and healings were reported.

VII Exposition: 3 December 1922 to 7 January 1923

The Exposition was held for the third centenary of the canonisation of St.

Francis Xavier. Large pilgrimages were organised by different dioceses and more than 25, 000 people were present on the opening day, about 4000 masses were celebrated during this Exposition and in all 5,00,000 venerated the sacred Relic.

VIII Exposition: 3 December 1931 to 10 January 1932

General Joao Carlos Craveiro Lopes took over as the new Governor of Goa and he wanted to start his duties as a Governor with an Exposition of the Body. Dr. Wolfango da Silva, the Director of Health Services, in the presence of the Archbishop, examined the Relic and remarked that there was no change. More than 5,00,000 people venerated the sacred Relic.

IX Exposition: 6 to 17 May 1942

To mark the 400th year of arrival of St. Francis Xavier and also to celebrate the Episcopal Jubilee of Pope Pius XII on 13 May, an Exposition was authorised but because of the World War II, the Exposition was very simple and the pilgrims attending were fewer. During this Exposition, there were many requests to kiss the feet of the

Exposition photo of the relics of St. Francis Xavier 1984-85

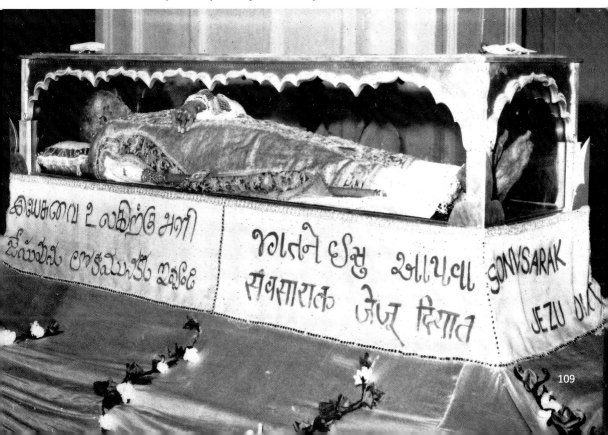

Exposition photo of the relics of St. Francis Xavier 1984-85

saint. Msgr Francisco da Piedade Rebelo, Secretary of the Patriarcado, issued an announcement granting the permission to the pilgrims to kiss the feet of the saint during this Exposition.

X Exposition: 3 December 1952 to 6 January 1953

This Exposition was held to mark the occasion of the 400th death anniversary of St. Francis Xavier. The Indian Postal department released three commemorative stamps and postcards. The relic was examined by Dr. Antonio de Sousa Sobrinho, Director of Health Services and Dr. Joao Manuel Pacheco de Figueiredo, Director of Medical School and nothing had changed in the Relic.

At the end of this Exposition, it was decided that the Relic should no longer be touched by the pilgrims directly; so it was enclosed in a crystal urn in 1955.

XI Exposition: 14 to 31 December 1961

The Indian Army entered Goa on 18 December and freed Goa from the Portuguese control on 19 December 1961. The Exposition was then taking place in the shadow of the war and the visitors were lesser than before. The victorious Indian soldiery venerated the body of the saint before returning to their base. The Relics were quietly put back into the glass case by the Indian Army.

XII Exposition: 24 November 1964 to 6 January 1965

The thirty-eight International Eucharistic Congress was held in Bombay from 28 November to 6 December 1964. Pope Paul VI had attended this Congress and the Exposition of the Relic of the saint was held from 24 November to 6 the

Exposition of the relics of St. Francis Xavier 1994-95

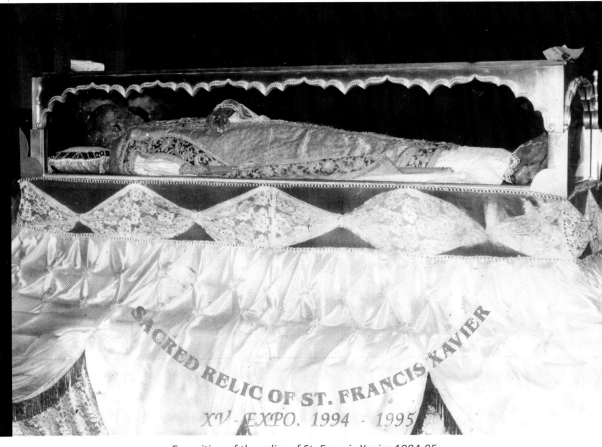

Exposition of the relics of St. Francis Xavier 1994-95

January 1965. During this Exposition, three cardinals, twenty-four Bishops from abroad and nineteen from different parts of India came to venerate the sacred Relic and there were about 5,20,000 devotees. There were false rumours started by vested interests that the Relic would no longer be seen, so there was a continual influx of pilgrims especially from Bombay. Not to disappoint them, the glass case was left in the sacristy of Bom Jesus from

7 January, then it was placed in the silver casket on the marble Mausoleum, where a glimpse of the face could be seen from a distance. The definitive closure of the relic took place on 20 January 1965.

XIII Exposition: 23 November 1974 to 5 January 1975

On 12 February 1975, Dr. Joao Manuel Pacheco de Figueiredo, Ex-Dean of the Medical College, Panjim, and Dr. Pedro de

Ataide, physician, examined the sacred remains through the glass case for about half an hour, the Dean examining it for the third time. They found greater changes in the face: the left eye no longer protruded; the eyelids could still be distinguished. On the exterior, part of the face had skin which seemed to be dry, withered and rough with some spots of decay, and the hair of the beard was sticking to the chin. In the angle of the lower jaw there was a spot of decay in the skin, revealing clearly the bone in a fresh condition. The outer right ear looked rather atrophied. In the hand and the feet they could still see the flexuous veins and tendons. The right heel was detached but kept in position with the rest of the bones by a piece of wire. The colour of the skin of the parts that were bare was clayish.

Exposition of the relic of St. Francis Xavier 2004-05

Cleaning of the coffin of the relic of St. Francis Xavier, Bom Jesus Basilica

Pope Paul VI declared 1975 as the Holy Year, and the theme of this Exposition was "Love one another as I have loved you". The Exposition was opened by Joseph Cardinal Parecattil, Archbishop of Ernakulam. He was also the President of the Catholic Bishops' Conference of India. It was closed by the Apostolic Pro-Nuncio in India. Over 869,221 kissed the sacred Relic of the saint.

XIV Exposition: 21 November 1984 to 13 January 1985

This time the Exposition took place at the Cathedral of Goa. The theme of the Exposition was "Give the World Jesus". The main celebrant at the Inaugural Mass was Cardinal Joseph Cordeiro, Archbishop of Karachi. During this Exposition about 11,29.017 people venerated the sacred Relic of St. Francis Xavier.

XV Exposition: 21 November 1994 to 7 January 1995

The Exposition had the theme "For the family, For Society, For God". Around 19,78,174 pilgrims visited the Relic. Cardinal Simon Pimenta, then the

Archbishop of Mumbai, was the main celebrant for the opening ceremony.

XVI Exposition: 21 November 2004 to 2 January 2005

This Exposition was announced by the Archbishop of Goa before his retirement. The Archbishop of Goa and Daman, Reverend Filipe Neri Ferrao, was the main celebrant on 21 November 2004. There about 400 priests concelebrating the inaugural ceremony. After the mass, the glass case containing the Relic was carried to the Cathedral in a procession for veneration. More than 30,00,000 pilgrims venerated the sacred Relic of St. Francis Xavier and it was broadcast by local and international television.

XVII Exposition: 22 November 2014 to 4 January 2015

Archbishop Filipe Neri Ferrao issued the Decree confirming the holding of the solemn event, which will last for 44 days.

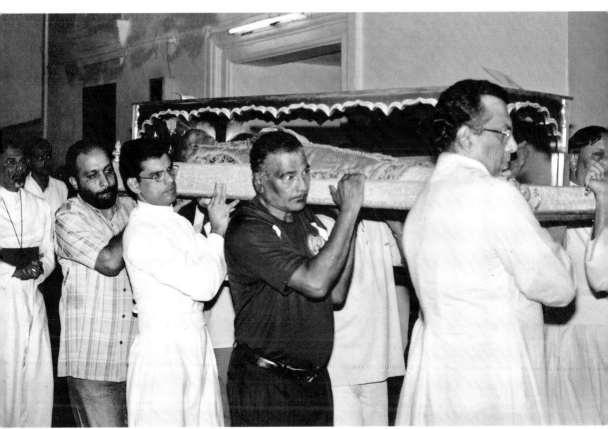

Carrying the coffin to the Nave of Bom Jesus Basilica

Acknowledgements

First and foremost, I would like to thank my parents, Pedro Camilo Lobo and Teresa da Costa Lobo, for inculcating religious values in me, my sister, Adelina Lobo Olivera for her overall unstinted support, my brother, Agnelo Lobo for photographic illustrations in this book. I also wish to place on record my gratitude to my beloved Bianca A. Rebello for inspiring and motivating me to write this book, giving me moral support and standing by me in difficult time during the journey of writing this book.

My sincere thanks to Archbishop-Patriarch Filipe Neri Ferrão for granting *Imprimatur* and Fr. Manuel Pascoal Gomes for *Nihil Obstat*.

I also like to extend my thanks to Fr. Francisco Caldeira for having gone through the text to give an inspiring foreword to this Book and Fr. Carmo Martins for his never-ending support.

Finally I also like to thank *Xavier Centre of Historical Research* and Librarian, Arti Fernandes. Les Menezes and Dr. Joe D' Souza for offering invaluable suggestions and helping me with critical appreciation.

Bibliography

Albuquerque, Viriato A. C. B. de, Exposicao do venerando corpo do glorioso apostolo das Indias, em 1890, Nova Goa, Imprensa Nacional, 1891 (on the exposition held in 1890)

Anuario de S. Francisco Xavier: orgao do seu santuario em Goa, Old Goa Bom Jesus Basilica, 1957-1961, 5 Vols (Annual Publication)

Bellessort, Andre, Voyages de Saint Francois Xavier, Flammarion, 1935

Bouhours, Domnic, The Life of St. Francis Xavier, of the Society of Jesus, Apostle of India, Published By Eugene Cummiskey, 130 South Sixth Street, 1841

Branganca-Pereira, A. B. De, S. Francisco Xavier: esboco historic, Nova Goa, Reparticao Central de Estatistica e Informacao, 1955

Brordrick, James, Saint Francis Xavier (1506 – 1552), London, Burns & Oates, 1952

Caraman, Philip, Ignatius Loyola – A Biography of the Founder of the Jesuits, New York, Harper & Row, 1990

Carretto, Carlo, I, Francis, J. Njarakkatt at St. Paul Press Training School, 2005

Coleridge, Henry James, The Life and letters of St. Francis Xavier, 3rd ed., 2 vols., London, Burns & Oates, 1902

Correia-Afonso, Francisco, The spirit of Xavier, pref. A. Goodier, Bangalore, Good Shepherd Convent Press, 1922

Correia-Afonso, John, Even unto the Indies -   Ignatius of Loyola and the Indian Mission, Bombay, The Messenger of the Sacred Heart, 1956

Costa, Francisco Xavier da, Exposicao do venerando corpo de S. Francisco Xavier em 1931, Nova Goa, Tip. of "A Voz de S. Francisco Xavier", 1935

Costa, Francisco Xavier da, Exposicao do venerando corpo de S. Francisco Xavier em 1900-1910-1922: resumo historico, Nova Goa, Tip. Braganca, 1924

Costa, Francisco Xavier da, Resumo historico da exposicao das sagradas reliquias de S. Fancisco Xavier, em 1952, Bastora, Tip. Rangel, 1954

Dalmases, Candido de, Ignatius of Loyola, Founder of the Jesuits – his life and work, Anand, Gujarat Sahitya Prakash, 1985

Daurignac, J. M. S., S. Francisco Xavier: apostolo das Indias, 5th ed., Porto, Livraria Apsotolado da Imprensa, 1959

Devas, Dominic, St. Francis of Assisi, London, Catholic Truth Society, 1950

Don Peter, W. L. A., Francis Xavier, teacher of the nations, Colombo, Evangel Press, 1987

Exposition of St. Francis Xavier – 23rd November 1974 – 5th January 1975, Panjim, Tip. Prafulla, 1975

Fernandes, I. P. Newman, St. Francis Xavier and Old Goa, Quepem, Koinia Publication, 1994 (Guide book with biographical sketch)

Fonseca, Jose Nicolau Da, An Historical and Archaeological Sketch of the City of Goa, Thacker & C.O, Limited, 1878

Gracias, Fatima Silva da, St. Francis Xavier. His Memories in Goa, Lisboa, 2004 (Offprint)

Habig Marion A, St. Francis of Assisi, writings and early Biographies: English Omnibus of the Sources for the Life of St. Francis, Franciscan Herald Press, 1972

Jou, Albert, The Saint on mission: the story of St. Francis Xavier, Anand (Gujarat), Sahitya Prakash, 1984

Lobo, Patrick J, Magnificent Monuments of Old Goa, Rajhauns Vitaran, Panjim, 2004

Loyola Furtado, Miguel (Max), O grande apostolo do seculo XVI, Margao, Tip. of "A India Portuguesa", 1910

Lucena, J. de, Vida do padre Francisco de Xavier (Historia da vida), fac-sim ed. 2 vols, Lisboa, Agencia Geral do Ultramar, 1952

Mendes, Alvaro Renato, The Life of Francis Xavier, Panjim, Casa Fernandes, 1968

Mendonca, Delio de, Saint Francis Xavier in India, New Age Printers, Verna, Salcete, Goa

Mores, George Mark, St. Francis Xavier Apostolic Nuncio, Bombay, Konkan Institute of Arts and Science, 1952

Narayan, Rajan, Goencho Saib – The life and mission of St. Francis Xavier, Panjim, Tata Press Ltd., 1994

Paes, James S., Flame in the Indies - The Life of Saint Francis Xavier, Margao, Sheth Publishers

Rayanna, P., St. Francis Xavier and his shrine, 3rd ed., rev. Moreno de Souza, Old Goa, Bom Jesus Basilica, 1998

Recondo, Jose Maria, Castillo de Javier, illus. Jesus Maria Munarriz, Barcelona, FISA Industrias Gracficas, 1998 (On his castle in Spain)

Schurhammer, G., Francis Xavier: his life, his times, trans. From German M. Joseph Costeloe, 4 vols., Rome, The Jesuit Historical Institute, 1973 – 1980 (vol.I Europe, v.2 India, v.3 Indonesia & v.4 Japan & China)

The Navhind Times – A commemorative issue on the life and work of St. Francis Xavier (The Exposition of the Relics of St. Francis Xavier 2004), ed. By Arun Sinha, Panaji, Vilas V. Sardessai, 2004

The works of John Dryden – Prose – The Life of St. Francis Xavier 1688, ed. By Alan Roper, London, University of California Press, 1979

Thompson, Francis, St. Ignatius Loyola, London, Burns & Oates, 1962